we will ♪urvive

True Stories of Encouragement, Inspiration, and the Power of Song

GLORIA GAYNOR and SUE CARSWELL

we will survive

survive

True Stories of Encouragement, Inspiration, and the Power of Song

GLORIA GAYNOR and SUE CARSWELL

GRAND HARBOR PRESS

Published by Grand Harbor Press
1704 Eaton Drive
Grand Haven, MI 49417

ISBN13: 9781477848036
ISBN10: 1477848037

"I Will Survive"
Written by Dino Fekaris and Frederick Perren
Universal-PolyGram International Publishing, Inc. on behalf of itself and
Perren-Vibes Music, Inc.
Used by Permission - All Rights Reserved

We Will Survive is a work of memoir. It reflects the authors' present
recollections of their experiences over a period of years. Certain names,
locations, and identifying characteristics have been changed. Dialogue
and events have been recreated from memory, and, in some cases,
have been compressed to convey the substance of what was said or
what occurred.

We dedicate this book to all of us who have been physically, emotionally, mentally, and spiritually scarred by life's trials and tribulations but are brave enough to survive the storms with courage and tenacity and forge ahead to victory.

I WILL SURVIVE

At first I was afraid, I was petrified
Kept thinkin' I could never live without you by my side
Then I spent so many nights thinking, how you did me wrong
And I grew strong and I learned how to get along

And so you're back from outer space
I just walked in to find you here
With that sad look upon your face
I should have changed that stupid lock
I should have made you leave your key
If I had known for just one second you'd be back to bother me

Go on now, go walk out the door
Just turn around now 'coz you're not welcome anymore
Weren't you the one who tried to break me with goodbye?
Did you think I'd crumble? Did you think I'd lay down and die?

Oh, no not I, I will survive
For as long as I know how to love, I know I'll stay alive
I've got all my life to live and I've got all my love to give
I'll survive, I will survive, hey, hey

It took all the strength I had not to fall apart
Just trying hard to mend the pieces of my broken heart
And I spent oh, so many nights just feeling sorry for myself
I used to cry, but now I hold my head up high

And you see me, somebody new
I'm not that chained up little person still in love with you
And so you felt like dropping in and just expect me to be free
But now I'm savin' all my lovin' for someone who's lovin' me

Go on now, go walk out the door
Just turn around now you're not welcome anymore
Weren't you the one who tried to break me with goodbye
Did you think I'd crumble? Did you think I'd lay down and die?

Oh, no not I, I will survive
Oh, as long as I know how to love, I know I'll stay alive
I've got all my life to live and I've got all my love to give
I'll survive, I will survive, hey hey

Go now, go walk out the door
Just turn around now 'coz you're not welcome anymore
Weren't you the one who tried to break me with goodbye?
Did you think I'd crumble? Did you think I'd lay down and die?

Oh, no not I, I will survive
Oh, as long as I know how to love, I know I'll stay alive
I've got all my life to live and I've got all my love to give
I'll survive, I will survive, I will survive

CONTENTS

PROLOGUE

Over the years I have been told countless stories regarding the wonderful effects "I Will Survive" has had on people. While I expected it to touch many people, I never imagined the far-reaching responses from every nationality, race, creed, color, and age group it has produced. One of my favorite stories—and perhaps among the most touching—was told to me while I was on one of my many trips to Italy.

I had become a born-again Christian just before I recorded "I Will Survive" and felt I should change the lyrics to reflect the foundation on which the song stood for me. Originally, the line was: "It took all the strength I had not to fall apart." I changed it to "Only the Lord could give me strength not to fall apart."

At the end of a show, I sang "I Will Survive" with the new words for the first time. Afterward, a young Asian girl came up to me to say how much she had enjoyed the concert. She told me she had intended to go home that morning but had missed her flight.

"I'm so sorry," I said.

"I'm not," the girl replied. "I believe God caused me to miss my flight so that I could see your show."

I thought, *that's really sweet,* but my hand came up to cover my wide-open mouth and I looked at her in astonishment as she continued: "A lot of problems that I've been suffering with have caused me to be really depressed recently. I don't have any privacy where I'm living here in Italy, so I was going home so that I could commit suicide."

Tears welled up in both our eyes as we embraced and thanked God that He had brought the three of us together: two strangers and a song—an anthem, a mantra and, now, a lifesaver.

That's the gift that I have been given and the wonderful privilege I've had of sharing with the world. This is my song, my mission, my one beautiful purpose in my life . . . my honor.

—Gloria Gaynor
June 2013

INTRODUCTION

Behind the Song

I grew up in a single-parent home with a single mother and six siblings—therein lay the crux of my problems. Too few people know the devastating long-term effects that can ravage the life of a child raised without a father—or at least a good father figure. I had no uncles—my mother was an only child—and my father had two sisters but no brothers.

When I was five years old, we moved from an apartment building to a two-family house. There was a young, childless couple, John and Mary, who lived on the second floor. I often visited them, and they played with me every day.

One day Mary went to the hospital to deliver their first child. I had come to think of them as an aunt and uncle, so it was not strange to me when John invited me up to their apartment to have cookies and milk. I innocently allowed him to lead me into the bedroom, where he proceeded to lift me onto the bed and remove my panties. As he began to molest me, I looked up at him and said, "My mommy's not gonna like this!"

He responded angrily: "Your mother's not gonna know!"

"Yes, she will, cuz I'll tell her," I timidly said.

At that he hurriedly replaced my panties, snatched me from the bed, and dragged me to the front door of the apartment, where he shoved me out with a growl: "Git on back downstairs. You make me sick." Looking back on it now, I think he probably meant, "You make me scared."

My mother was a no-nonsense, take-no-crap-from-anyone kind of person, and John knew it. Because of that, I never told her what happened that day. I believed she would probably have hurt him seriously, which would have meant jail time and that I would be left without a mother as well as a father. I had no way of realizing then that John had stolen my innocence that afternoon and had reinforced the low self-esteem and abandonment issues I already suffered, born of fatherlessness.

Fatherlessness, coupled with this incident, set the stage for my behavior in male relationships from then on. I grew up feeling that every rejection or maltreatment from any man for any reason was because I wasn't worthy of better treatment. When I was twelve, my mother had a relationship with a man she grew to love. For two years she kept him away from my siblings and me, so as not to have someone around who might, in some way, harm her daughters. Eventually he came to live with us, and we grew to like him a lot. He was a father figure—until one day he sexually molested me while I was asleep in my bedroom and my mother was asleep in hers.

"Why are you doing this?" I asked as I awoke.

"I was just trying to see if you were messing with those little boys," he answered.

"You could have asked me that," I snapped back.

I stopped him before he had gone too far, but the damage to my psyche had already been done. Again I didn't tell my mom, even though her greatest fear had come to pass. I had seen her alone and lonely for years, and I didn't want to get in the way of her happiness with the man she loved. I also didn't want her to get into trouble for trying to seek retribution against him.

The incidents with my stepfather and John, as well as my reactions to them, set the tone for my future relationships with men and became par for the course. I ended up being rejected, disrespected, and neglected in every relationship, from puberty up to and including my marriage. When I was eighteen, I was naïve enough to trust the cousin of an ex-boyfriend. I allowed him to take me to visit his girlfriend—only to find that not only was she not home, there was no one there at all. He raped me. "Don't even think of screaming," he threatened. "No one else is here, no one will hear you, and you will only piss me off. So, act like you like it!"

When I got home that night, I went straight to the bathroom and tried to scrub away the guilt and shame I felt. It did not work. I never told anyone about it because, again, I didn't want anyone to get in trouble for trying to defend me. Legal recourse never crossed my mind. Again, I just considered it all par for the course.

When I met my husband, Linwood, I thought he was my knight in shining armor. He was handsome, intelligent, gallant, chivalrous, generous, and so much fun. After two years I made him my manager. As artist/girlfriend and manager/boyfriend, our relationship was great for two years that was followed by a not-so-terrific one.

In the midst of my trouble in paradise, I received a notice from my record company. For no apparent reason, they were not renewing my recording contract, which would expire at the end of the year.

One night, at one of my shows, I had an accident onstage and woke up the next morning paralyzed from the waist down. I ended up in the hospital for spinal surgery. People were going around the record company saying, "The Queen is dead." Was I simply a one-hit wonder with "Never Can Say Goodbye"? During the three-month hospital stay that followed, God got my attention. Gripped with fear of abandonment, physical handicap, and showbiz obscurity, I reached out to Him for help.

True to form, the Lord didn't fail me. Within a year I had a massive hit with "I Will Survive," and Linwood and I were married. Like so many innocent women, I thought, *now that we're married, things will be different; our focus will be on building a happy family together.* I wasn't the perfect wife, but I was attentive, trusting, reassuring, supportive, affectionate, loving, caring, and faithful. Linwood wasn't all that bad as a husband. He was supportive as far as my career was concerned—physically protective and affectionate. But he took disrespect and disregard to a whole new level. I think he became so self-absorbed that he didn't care if he was being hurtful to me. He had no concept of commitment and thought a grown man should be free to do whatever he wanted, stay out all night as many nights as he liked—so he did. It's enough to say, as I often do, that I stayed at that party way too long.

What Linwood didn't count on was the impact of "I Will Survive" and how much it would do for me. When I recorded the song, I thought of it concerning the courage it produced in me regarding my career, my mom's passing, and the surgery I'd just had, and how it would encourage and inspire other people as well.

Now it became my mantra. It guided me in holding on to my faith and trusting God to bring me victoriously through all my trials and tribulations. I learned that internal scars—like those caused by father-lessness, my stepfather, my ex-boyfriend's cousin, and Linwood—put holes in your soul. Those scars can be just as deep as physical ones. They are just as painful and damaging, and generally hurt longer and are more debilitating. It took a while, but I grew strong, and I truly learned how to get along. My courage grew, and I began to recognize my own strength and the power God had placed in me. I spent several more years trying to make my marriage successful. But, as I told my husband on several occasions, "The problem with pushing a person to her limit is that no one knows what her limit is until she reaches it, and then it's too late."

Indeed, it became too late. I had reached my limit and came to the conclusion I couldn't make the marriage work on my own and it was time to end it. My husband had taken up permanent residence in the state of denial and it was time for me to make a move as well. When I told my pastor I was getting a divorce, he asked me how I felt about it. After a long pause, I said, "Free at last, free at last, thank God Almighty, I'm free at last!"

I never missed Linwood because, to tell the truth, he had left me years before the divorce. But it was great getting to know the new me, the *me* so many abusive men had caused to hide deep down inside.

Well, she's out now. I love her, and God loves her, and she'll never go into hiding again.

Indeed, I will survive.

...

In the following pages, you will find compelling stories that will likely mirror the experiences of yourself, family members, friends, and acquaintances. They are real-life stories of real people who valiantly climbed mountains of seemingly insurmountable obstacles to reach the pinnacle of triumph.

This book came about in a special way. My team—Sue Carswell, Stephanie Gold (my manager), and I—put out the word across the world that we were looking for survival stories for this book. We eventually received stories from as far away as Africa—including one story of a woman who was encamped in Auschwitz, another from a 9/11 mother, and the story of an autistic boy ordering flowers for his mother for Mother's Day. We contacted blogs and writing magazines and reached out to various organizations that had members' stories depicting the true essence of the song. Several of these groups included healing resources for abused women and men. It seems we used every connection we could find. Some in this book are even our friends' stories. In the end we narrowed it down to forty stories we felt best illuminated the lyrics of my song. They vary in dimension, but I am very proud of each and every contributor for making this book come true.

My sincere hope is that these stories will provide inspiration, encouragement, and empowerment to you—no matter what challenges you might be facing. If the remarkable people in these stories can survive as I did, I know you can too!

MOTHER CUB LOVE
by Susan Lynn Perry

Ding dong! The doorbell rang loudly on a Sunday afternoon. It was Mother's Day, and I had already been showered with beautiful flowers by my husband, a sweet basket of tasty treats by my parents, and a big hug and special kiss by my young son.

I opened the door to find a deliveryman standing there with an enormous vase full of multicolored roses. Completely perplexed, I turned to my husband to see if he knew who they were from. He shrugged his shoulders and helped me carry the vase into the kitchen, eager to see who had sent me such a thoughtful gift. He set the vase down and handed me the envelope, which I quickly opened. I read out loud: "Happy Mother's Day—to the best mom in the whole wide world."

I looked up at my husband, who was just as confused as I was. Then I turned to my son, who had just come running into the kitchen with a smile on his face that stretched from ear to ear. "These are from you?" I asked.

"Uh-huh. Do you like them?" I had never seen such a happy, proud look on his face.

"I love them! But how . . ."

"It was so easy," he said, interrupting me. "It was just like the commercial said. I went to the computer, typed in the Web site, and ordered the biggest vase of flowers I could find. I even paid extra for the special Sunday delivery! And I got you the chocolates and bath salts too! And the best part was I didn't even have to pay for them!" (Apparently, my credit-card information had been saved from the last time I had ordered flowers. I made a mental note to immediately delete that information.)

Now I know you might be thinking that this is a really cute story of the wonderful bond between a mother and her son. And you're right. But what makes this all the more special is that just a few years earlier, my son had been diagnosed with autism. I was told flat out by his pediatrician: "Your son has autism. There is no cure. He will probably never be able to show love like other people do. His health and mental status will continue to decline over the coming years, and you will probably have to institutionalize him at some point."

Hard to believe we're talking about the same child, isn't it?

My beautiful, healthy baby boy—who had developed perfectly in his first year of life—eventually regressed into a vacant world full of pain, suffering, and an inability to communicate with others. I spent the next six years deep in the trenches, struggling to help him find his way back to us. I spent many nights crying myself to sleep, thinking there was no way I could survive the overwhelming challenge I faced.

His medical and dietary needs were never ending. There were doctors' appointments, therapy consultations, countless hours on the computer, meetings with teachers, stacks of books and research materials, newly discovered supplements, special foods to accommodate his dietary needs, medications and shots, and on and on. There were no clear answers but an awful lot of conflicting theories and information on proper treatment. The recovery process began slowly and for every positive step forward, there would be a huge regression looming right around the corner. As you can imagine, this made it very hard to proceed with much optimism and hope. And even though the path was arduous and exhausting at best, I can clearly remember the turning point that drove me to keep moving onward.

One day, after a particularly long and difficult week of crazy, erratic behavior from my son—we had been diligently working to rebalance his delicate gastrointestinal issues—he had such explosive diarrhea that he left a trail of it from the living room through the kitchen and all the way into the bathroom. When I came out of my bedroom and saw the awful mess, I sank to the floor, giving up in total despair. I was exhausted, sleep deprived, and so emotionally drained I did not think I could go on. I knew my son needed me desperately, but I had nothing left to give.

Thankfully, my husband saw what had happened and picked me up, marched me back into our bedroom, and instructed me not to come out again until he had taken care of everything. He closed the door and proceeded to clean up the disaster while I retreated to our bathroom and completely shut down. I was done. There was just no way I could take another day. I turned on the hot water, threw in some bath salts, and lit several candles. I turned on the radio and melted into the bubbly warmth, sobbing hysterically. I felt like such a failure, like all of my sacrifices and efforts had gotten us nowhere. After a few minutes, my emotions finally started to subside. And that's when it happened.

Gloria Gaynor's song "I Will Survive" came blasting out of the speakers, as if on cue, as if I had called the station myself and requested it. The words filled my soul, giving me the strength I so desperately needed to clear my head and organize my scrambled thoughts into a plan of action: "I'm not going to give up and die. I will survive too!" Although Ms. Gaynor was talking about a totally different personal tragedy, her words reached out and grabbed me, rescuing me from my dark thoughts.

I realized at that very moment that I needed to do three things. First, I needed to educate myself. I had been so eager to help my boy that I had grabbed hold of every book, article, magazine, and Web site I could find—only to overwhelm myself to the point of giving up. I needed to slow down, make a list, and learn as much as I could about each complicated aspect of his condition—one at a time.

Second, I knew I needed to share my journey with others who might be going through the same thing. With so much conflicting information from the "expert" doctors, therapists, and researchers, I knew there were many other parents out there who were probably on the verge of giving up just like me. I decided at that moment that it was up to me to be strong for my boy and for the countless other children and parents who were in the same position.

And third, I knew I needed to carve out some time to take care of myself too. (This part is still a work in progress.) After all, how could I possibly be around long enough to take care of my son if I was running myself into the ground? I resolved then and there to focus at least part of my efforts on my own mental and physical wellness.

Flash forward to today, when both mother and cub have indeed survived. I took that plan, inspired by the song, and moved forward with a vengeance. I didn't give up. I fought hard for my son, myself, and my family. We're not perfect now and we might never be, but there is a bond between us that will never be broken. In fact, that bond was never more apparent than a few nights ago, when I was putting my sweet boy to bed. As I gave him his hugs and kisses, he looked me in the eye and said the most precious words: "You know what, Mom? I will never love anyone more than I love you. I just thought you should know that."

These words from a boy who the doctors said would never be able to show me love. I now no longer doubt if we will survive. I know we will because Gloria told me so. And you know what? She was right.

ANNIE TWICE CHOSEN

by Annie Bleiberg

I was born October 1, 1920, to a middle-class Zionist family in Oleszyce, Poland. My father bought and sold cowhides to tanneries, and my mother was a homemaker. I had one sister named Helen, who was five years younger than me. My parents always wished for a boy because only males were allowed to say kaddish (the mourner's prayer). I never thought that was fair, and I had no problem voicing my opinion. I believed in equal rights. I was an excellent student, as my parents enforced that in us. My mother always said that we could do anything we wanted as long as we were educated, and education would help us throughout our lives. We lived in a very mixed neighborhood of Jews and Catholics, and I had a lot of friends.

I experienced my first episode of antisemitism in school, when one of my favorite professors said that all Jews should be pushed into the Baltic Sea. Surprised and horrified, several Jewish students started to cry. Soon afterwards, things began changing for the Jews.

We all had heard of Hitler before 1933, but mostly that he was trying to rise in politics. We had no idea of his calculated plan over the years to execute a mass destruction of all European Jews. How could anyone ever get away with this? How could the world watch and not help? We were forced out of our homes in Jaroslaw, Poland, and my parents moved us into my grandfather's house in Oleszyce, as he lived on the border of Poland and Russia. Hitler decided to expel all Jews to the Russians.

In September 1938 Germany and Russia signed an agreement to jointly invade, divide, and occupy Poland. The Soviets deported many

Jews who fell in their occupation zone to Siberia. In 1939 we were not sent east and remained in Oleszyce, but every personal belonging of any value that we had was taken away by the Russians, except for a watch I hid. I knew I might need it later on.

In June 1941, Hitler broke his pact with the Soviets and invaded Russian territory. The Germans burned our synagogues to the ground. We had to live a life in hiding, and if we dared go outside, we had to be very careful. People were afraid to help the Jews, as they were afraid of being killed themselves. In 1942, Jews were being forcibly deported to the ghettos in Lubaczów. There was no food, no heat, and we slept on cold floors. Dead bodies were everywhere. Many of us hid in secret spaces or underground bunkers as long as we could, and hoped the war would end soon. My will to live was enormous. Many did not have the strength and committed suicide.

A kind Catholic family helped us, bringing us a little food, but they had to be so careful because if they were caught helping Jews, the whole family would have been executed. They had to stop bringing us food when snow fell, as their footprints could be traced back to our hiding place. My sister was not as healthy as me, and my mom got sick. My dad was able to get out to try to find better housing for us, as he knew my mom and sister would not make it if we stayed where we were. He was not successful. We were forced into cattle cars and deported to the Belzec death camp. My father was able to smuggle some tools onto the train, and he pried off a few wooden slats so people could jump out. Men started to jump off the moving train, and my mother was able to push me out. That was the last time I ever felt my mother's touch. My mother and sister did not get off. I often wonder what my sister thought when my mother picked me to save. I imagine she knew she and my sister were not strong enough to make it. She knew I had the will and tenacity to survive.

I was lucky to have fallen into a snow heap but lay unconscious for a while after the jump from the moving train. My lack of movement proved very lucky for me as the Germans thought I was dead and moved on. I woke up from the sound of a gunshot nearby. I was able to get up and start walking. I remember my father telling me to walk in the opposite direction from the train. If the Poles turned us in they were rewarded, so I had to be very careful. I came across another Jewish woman, and together we began our journey. She knocked on many doors, but we were turned away; people were afraid to help. Finally a man let us in his home and gave us a potato. That was the best potato I ever had. He let us take a nap and then told us we had to leave. We went back to the ghetto, and it was then that I was miraculously reunited with my father, who had also jumped from the train. My father took us to a gentile family friend with whom we stayed for four weeks. He fed us but was also afraid of getting caught. My father wanted to go to another empty ghetto, but my tenacity for life began to fade. I felt hopeless. I wanted to turn myself in to the Gestapo.

My father found friends of my grandfather who worked for the Polish underground. They made us fake Polish "Aryan" papers so we could work as slaves in Germany. With the false documents, I was able to board a train with other Poles being sent to Germany for labor. On the train I was betrayed by someone who knew me and was beaten to a state of unconsciousness. I was separated from my father and later discovered that he had been sent to a slave labor camp.

In the police station, I offered a policeman the only thing I had left, my watch, if he would let me go. He told me to keep it. It was then that I was sent to Auschwitz-Birkenau. When we arrived the guards separated people by gender. They sent the ill, the old, the children, and the pregnant women to the gas chambers. They selected other people to be slaves. I was one of the lucky ones. They cut our hair, put us in showers, and we were tattooed. My number was, and is, 38330. I smelled the dead bodies that were burned. The smell filled the air. The gas chambers were built to look like showers, so many thought they were being allowed to bathe. But it was a trick, as the gas fumes came out of the showerheads. It really was a miracle I was spared. I now know it was because I was meant to live to tell the story and be the voice of millions.

In Auschwitz-Birkenau they woke us up at 5:00 A.M. to start our workday. If we found any food and tried to eat it, we were beaten or bitten by dogs. We received the bare minimum to keep us alive. Once a month we had to strip in front of the guards to make sure we looked healthy enough; otherwise we were killed. This went on for a year and a half as we prayed the war would end.

As the Soviet Army made its way west, prisoners were forced onto death marches. My death march ended up in a labor camp near Prague. When the Russians finally liberated us, we shouted out in joy, many of us crying and hugging one another, but all our loved ones had been murdered. We left in small groups on trains to Prague, where there were relief organizations like the American Jewish Joint Distribution Committee (JDC) and the Red Cross. The JDC helped us with food and clothing. It was there that I saw a man I knew, who later was the man I would marry. He told me my father was still alive and living in my grandfather's house. I decided to take a train there, only to find out my father had learned I was still alive and left to look for me. We finally found each other. We were all we had left. The war was over, but the pain and memories will be etched in my brain as the tattoo is on my arm. My dad and I moved to another place in Poland, where my future husband was also living. We got married and moved to Germany, hoping we could emigrate to America. My father stayed in Poland.

My husband and I had one daughter and eventually were able to move to the USA. My husband became a tailor and then a builder, and I became a junior accountant after taking classes. It was very important for me to learn to speak English well. We lived in the Bronx for forty years, near Pelham Parkway.

In 1978 I lost my husband to cancer. Soon after, a song was playing on the radio called "I Will Survive." The lyrics echoed in me as I listened, wondering how they could portray parts of my life.

My daughter is married and lives on Long Island, and I'm very proud to say that she is a professor of sociology at Dowling College. She has three grown children. She wanted me to move to Long Island, but I did not want to go because I had been forced to move around so much during the Holocaust. Eventually I did move near her to keep her happy.

Years later, my daughter and granddaughter went with me back to Germany, to see the monument at the Belzec death camp. It is very hard for my granddaughter to comprehend the tragedy, and she says if this happened to her grandma, it could happen anywhere, anytime, anyplace. It has been my life's mission to make sure it never happens again. I am ninety-two years old as of this writing, but there were many times during my life that I could have, should have died, but I was shown some kindness, escaped death, and endured unbearable hardships. I don't believe any of it was accidental; I was chosen as a Jew and, as my mother always said, I was given great strength of character, so I was chosen to give testimony about the atrocities that happened under the Nazis. I have been a speaker for the Holocaust Memorial and Tolerance Center of Nassau County in Glen Cove for many years. I love entertaining, I love people. I have three grandchildren, two great-grandchildren, and I have all my life to live and I have so much love to give and I WILL SURVIVE.

*In July 2013, Annie attended Gloria's concert, along with 10,000 others in Long Island. While singing "I Will Survive," Gloria did a shout-out to Annie as a survivor. They spoke after the show and continue to remain in touch.

EVELYN ON TOP

by Alice Muschany

Despite thirteen years of annual mammograms that were considered normal, at age forty-four I received devastating news. I had late-stage breast cancer.

At my first appointment, my oncologist explained that dense tissue had prevented malignant cells from being visible on my previous X-rays. As I absorbed the gravity of my situation, my heart sank. My husband, Roland, turned to me, and I could read the compassion in his eyes. Overcome with crippling fear, I leaned against him and felt his quiet strength.

A deluge of tears streamed down my face when we broke the news to our children. All I ever wanted was to be there for them, sharing the simple pleasures in life. The expressions on their faces said that was all they wanted as well.

Clouds of doubt overshadowed future hopes and dreams. I'd already pictured a Norman Rockwell setting for my older years—apple-cheeked grandchildren running free while Roland and I watched from our wraparound front porch.

Music from the stereo played softly in the background as my thoughts spiraled downward. When Gloria Gaynor sang "I Will Survive," I felt the lyrics spoke directly to me. The song became my mantra.

I loved my husband, I loved my children, and I loved my life, and I'd be danged if I was going down without a fight. At my next appointment, the doctor walked into the room, and I let him know I had no intention of giving up.

He smiled when I said, "Hit me with your best shot. I want to live."

He did just that. The first round of chemotherapy knocked me to my knees. Three days of paying homage to the porcelain god sent me to the hospital for fluids due to dehydration. On the way home, I told Roland, "It's all uphill from here."

Before the inevitable loss of my hair, I rushed out and bought a wig. When my hair began falling out in clumps, I gave in and plopped the wig on my head. Grinning, I couldn't decide if the person in the mirror looked more like Dear Abby or Dustin Hoffman in *Tootsie*.

Along with music, I used humor to get me through. At first co-workers didn't know how to react when I cracked jokes about my hairpiece. I warned them I looked just like Curly of the Three Stooges without it. They laughed when I told them I still plugged in my curling iron every morning out of habit.

One woman took me aside and asked, "How can you be so upbeat?"

"It's easy," I said. "I'm a survivor."

As I walked across the parking lot after lunch, gale-force winds had me holding on to my wig for dear life. Later the girl who sat across from me in the office suggested I look in a mirror. Sure enough, my wig was more than a little crooked. We both burst out laughing.

After only a few weeks, I ditched the itchy wig for a more comfortable turban. When my boss approached and asked if I'd mind coming up with a slogan for the United Way drive our company participated in annually, I pointed to my turban and said, "No problem. I've already got my thinking cap on."

One morning I glanced in the mirror and noticed my remaining eyebrows had begun to turn white, so I grabbed a dark eyebrow pencil and went to work. My family just shook their heads when I walked out displaying thick Groucho Marx brows.

For each and every treatment, I marched into the chemo room with a take-no-prisoners attitude. Doctors and nurses alike continually praised my positive outlook. As I sat down in the brown leather recliner to begin the chemo drip, the nurse would recite my motto before I could.

"There's our survivor," she would say with a smile.

During my long battle, my husband remained faithfully at my side. My caring family stood by me as well. Neighbors stepped forward to offer love, support, baked goods, and casseroles. Even people I barely knew cheered me on. I vowed to return the favors the first chance I got.

From the beginning my mailbox overflowed with encouraging cards. Some made me cry. Others made me laugh. My favorite had a picture of a hairy-faced werewolf standing next to a wishing well with the caption: "Bob got more than he bargained for when he wished for a full head of hair."

Months later, at my nephew's wedding reception, Evelyn—an elderly friend of my mother-in-law—had had a few too many drinks. Her ill-fitting dentures danced around in her mouth like a character in a scene from a Stephen King novel. When she leaned forward to speak, her bottom teeth fell out onto Roland's arm. We managed to save our laughter until the way home. But once we started, we couldn't quit and laughed until we cried. That's when Roland chose "Evelyn" as the code word to inform me when my wig needed rearranging. Just saying her name brought on fits of laughter.

Eventually radiation netted me a whole new medical staff that applauded my optimistic frame of mind. After just one week of treatments, everyone knew I planned on being around for a long time.

Two surgeries, six chemotherapy treatments, and thirty-five radiation sessions later, my oncologist uttered the sweetest words ever: "Congratulations! You're cancer-free."

Eighteen wonderful years have passed since my cancer diagnosis. With such a grave prognosis, many are amazed I'm doing so well.

Oh, no, not I, I will survive.

BEYOND SURVIVAL

by Darcy Keith

The stretch of road from Muncie, Indiana, to Morehead, Kentucky, is only 280 miles long—a drive normally lasting less than six hours. When I started out on that road as an ambitious college senior, little did I know that my life and dreams for the future would come to a screeching halt in a matter of hours—not to mention that two of my closest friends would be dead. Everything physically, mentally, emotionally, and financially that I had accomplished thus far in my short life was gone forever after the tragic accident that occurred on that road.

Or was it?

In early September of my senior year, four sorority sisters and I were asked by our national sorority to help start a new chapter at Morehead State University. Currently serving as rush chairman, I happily agreed. But after we completed the rush parties and were returning to Ball State that evening, something went terribly wrong. As we entered the southern outskirts of Cincinnati, the driver lost control of our vehicle in the wind shear from two passing semis. The car spun and we ended up sideways in the middle of the north-bound lanes of the highway, trapped in the path of an approaching Freightliner semi tractor trailer. The resulting impact was so great that our car's crumpled side panel bore the imprint of the semi's front license plate.

When the screeching and grinding came to a halt, the two girls buckled in the front seats were able to exit the car and walk away. The three unbuckled girls in the back, including myself, weren't so lucky. Two were killed instantly. The paramedics could not tell at first whether I had survived the crash because they couldn't find my pulse; they had to remove some of my nail polish to be sure. If I was dead, the color under my fingernails would have been blue. It was pink. Barely breathing and placed on life support, I was rushed by Life Flight helicopter to the University of Cincinnati Medical Center and admitted to the surgical critical-care unit.

The injuries I sustained were massive. Unconscious, I remained in a coma for six days with frontal lobe and left-brain injuries that paralyzed my body's right side. The doctors told my parents that the prognosis was grim. Damage to the left side of my brain had resulted in a significant loss of memory and impaired my motor skills. Brain bruising, bleeding, and swelling in my frontal lobe had caused brain cells to die and left a gaping hole. The damage was done, but the extent was still unknown. My family, who prayed while they waited, would learn more about my significant and life-altering deficits when I woke up.

I awoke from my coma completely petrified. With no control over my bodily functions, I endured the humiliation of wearing adult diapers. Due to the right extremity paralysis, getting around required the use of a wheelchair. Also paralyzed was my right vocal cord, which initially left me unable to speak. My right lung collapsed, and I experienced drop foot (the inability to move the ankle and toes upward in order to walk correctly). Eating was difficult as well, since I was unable to swallow. A feeding tube that went up my nose and down my throat to my stomach nourished me daily. When I was finally able to feed myself, I was put in a special feeding group to learn how to swallow again. Once I mastered the swallowing process, I graduated to eating "normal," everyday food.

It was during a session with all my therapists present that I learned of the car crash and the deaths of my two sorority sisters, Constance and Rhonda. As I sat in shock upon hearing the news, the therapists watched closely to see my reaction. As I sat in disbelief, I could only utter the words, "Why didn't I die?" No one replied except my mother, although to this day I can't recall what she said to me. I couldn't believe that they were dead, but the scars on my body reminded me that something terrible had happened.

At first, my only thoughts were of how I was going to survive my injuries. Gloria Gaynor's song "I Will Survive" became a daily mantra. Beside my hospital bed was a chart listing various tasks I would have to accomplish independently before I could be discharged. I refused to dwell on my injuries or give up hope. Completing each task became my new goal. With determination, I began relearning simple skills like brushing my teeth, dressing myself, tying my shoes, and going to the bathroom. I progressed to more complex skills like eating, walking, and behaving normally for someone my age. Occupational and speech therapy helped get my brain cognitively back on track. During physical therapy, I was like a bobblehead doll from lack of neck and trunk support when I was placed upright. When I started getting some feeling back from the paralysis, the pain was so intense that I whimpered continually. This feeling was like pins and needles constantly poking me in my arm and leg. But despite the excruciating pain, I learned how to stand and walk without falling over because of my balance issues. Slowly, one by one, each item on my bedside chart was accomplished and checked off.

Emotionally, though, I was still struggling. Having a brain injury is similar to having attention deficit disorder. I didn't have the attention span to focus on the information I wanted to remember. I couldn't concentrate enough to remember it, or recall what I just did. Damage to my brain's left lobe left me unable to remember my entire college major. When one of my college textbooks was placed on the table in front of me, I just looked at it with a blank stare. No longer could I perform the required math tasks needed for my actuarial-science college major. In fact, I couldn't remember anything related to the subject. Before the crash I was going to be walking onstage draped in a bright red cap and gown, ready to receive my diploma. Now, with college graduation just six months away, that was no longer an option for me. How was I going to provide for myself financially if I couldn't graduate from college and get a job? My self-esteem and self-confidence plummeted. It took all the strength I had not to fall apart.

Extremely upset and emotional, I searched for what options were available for my "new normal" status. Not only would I learn how to survive—I would thrive. I had all my life to live, and I was not about to throw it away after being given a second chance. I wasn't about to spend time feeling sorry for myself. Developing a memorable recipe for overcoming adversity and dealing with change, I set out on a mission to rebuild my life. My exercise routine consisted of brisk, long walks and light strength training. To mend and reengage my brain, I reenrolled in college under a new major and graduated a short year and a half later, as determined as ever. The company with which I had interned offered me a job in a different capacity.

Holding my head up high, I continued to grow and flourish with determination and a positive attitude. To turn a devastating situation into a positive one, I went on a mission to help others live better lives by sharing my formula for overcoming adversity and making good decisions by serving as a professional keynote speaker for various organizations, associations, and corporations.

College students often make some pretty poor choices. Had the three of us in the backseat thought about the consequences of not wearing our seat belts, Constance and Rhonda would still be with us—and I wouldn't have sustained my life-altering injuries. Instead, I had made a conscious effort not to wear one. The reason? I didn't want to wrinkle my clothes, since I was going to a party when I returned to college. Pretty lame decision, wasn't it? That choice nearly cost me my life, and unfortunately, Constance and Rhonda paid the ultimate price by losing theirs.

By retelling the story and the vital lessons I learned from this tragedy, I have been blessed with the opportunity not only to help countless individuals and organizations overcome adversity and successfully deal with change, but also keep Constance's and Rhonda's memories alive. Several NFL teams have invited me to present the "Traffic Education and Decision Making" module of the NFL Rookie

Success Program annually to their new rookie class. My story and the subsequent consequences of making a poor decision are "incredibly powerful" to the rookies because I was their age when I made that tragic and life-altering choice.

I choose to live each day to the fullest. I don't dwell on things I can't control, nor do I take a "victim" attitude. Despite the obstacles ahead, I choose to embrace them with perseverance and fortitude. I don't allow my ego to get the best of me but ask for help when I need it. All of these elements helped me become the professional speaker, author, leader, and advocate I am today. "I Will Survive" is forever a song by which I and countless others who are experiencing similar issues will chant to empower ourselves to overcome adversity and live full lives.

The stretch of road from Muncie, Indiana, to Morehead, Kentucky, is only 280 miles long—a drive normally lasting less than six hours. But while everything did come to a screeching halt for a time, my life was far from being over. In fact, it had just begun.

I LOVED LUCY

by Stephanie Gold

It had been six years since my last dog. The pain of putting a dog to sleep is one that cuts through your heart and that you *never* forget.

There was no way I was going to go through that again.

But then I was working in the city, single and carefree. Every day a little dachshund named C. J. greeted me at work. He belonged to someone in an office on the same floor as mine. He disliked everybody except me. I actually enjoyed watching him chase people down the hall, barking his little head off. It was then I discovered my instant love for dachshunds.

I began researching breeders on the Internet and developed a nice rapport with one in Connecticut. The breeder was about to have a litter of "doxies" and promised to put me on the waiting list for one. My heart was set on a boy, but she had three girls—two of which were already taken. She sent me a photo of the last one.

Lo and behold, I was hooked on the dog just from the picture. I drove up to Connecticut to get her, wondering the whole way if I was doing the right thing, knowing my life would change once again. Then again, I didn't care. I was adopting her and I was going to name her after my favorite actress, Lucille Ball.

Lucy was as nervous as could be during the long drive home. After all, I did take her away from the only family she knew—how dare I decide her fate!

When we arrived home, I decided to do what everyone told me to do: crate train Lucy. We did not even make it through the night. So much for dogs not pooping where they sleep. In the bath she went and in my bed she slept. In my opinion, there really is nothing better than having your dog sleep next to you. It was instant, mutual admiration. She wanted to be with me wherever I was, and I wanted her to be with me wherever I was. The closer, the better.

I decided I was going to take Lucy to work with me in the city. Have dog, will travel. I bought all the gear I needed: a Sherpa bag, Wee-Wee Pads, inflatable bowls, outfits for all seasons, diamond-studded collars, personalized bandannas—you name it, Lucy got it. She was my kid and I was going to spoil her rotten.

We did not last in the city for long. My boss's partner wasn't thrilled with her being there. Lucy was not the friendliest of doxies. Even though I had my own office, I decided it was best to move on, so I quit rather than leaving Lucy home alone for twelve hours a day.

Not long after, I received a call from an old friend who said she was getting divorced and needed help with her career. I happily obliged— but only if I could bring Lucy. We worked out of my friend's home, so it was a done deal. Lucy and my new boss warmed up to each other in a few weeks. Lucy was so happy going there that when we got close to her home she would run back and forth to each window of the car and start crying happily in anticipation of seeing her new friend. My new boss was tolerant of Lucy's faults, as Lucy would like to leave what I called "little presents" in different rooms of her home. Doxies are a hard breed to potty train. She even took some nibbles from a few of my friend's houseguests. In Lucy's mind, these were intruders, and her job was to protect us. She really could not wait for people to leave so she could be with just the two of us. Lucy went with us everywhere—planes, trains, cars, you name it. We had to travel a lot, since my boss was a well-known singer. Lucy loved singing with her. Who knew that Lucy's singing partner would be Gloria Gaynor!

Lucy did not mind plane rides, but on one trip she was getting a little restless in her Sherpa bag, which was under the seat in front of me. I used to keep my feet in the bag, so she would know that I was not leaving her. That time she wanted more than my feet. She was whining and trying hard to get out of the bag and onto my lap.

Sometimes flight attendants would be OK with her sitting on my lap. Well, not this trip. So Gloria and I waited for the right moment to put Lucy between the two of us. Gloria hid her with her coat and Lucy fell asleep until the end of the flight. Doxies really do rule the roost, and I will happily admit I was controlled by my four-legged little creature.

Lucy loved cats, and we would often visit my friend's mom, Lillian, who had three. They would scatter as soon as Lucy walked in; she loved chasing them throughout the house, and they did their best to outsmart her every move. She never hurt them. Lucy really just wanted to play, but you can't tell that to a cat.

We had a blissful and happy eight years together when suddenly Lucy started urinating and drinking excessively. I immediately took her to the doctor and tests were done. I will never forget the phone call on March 4, 2010, when the vet told me Lucy had diabetes. Sure, I knew people who had diabetes, but I did not have a clue what would be required of me having a diabetic dog. What did he mean I would have to give Lucy shots two times a day—the same time every day— no matter what? I could not even stand getting a shot myself. I cried even before the doctor walked into the room. What did he mean that if she did not eat, I would have to adjust her insulin? Were cataracts the only side effect?

It was then I decided to read everything I could about this disease and even joined support groups. I became obsessed with finding out everything I could to help Lucy. It took me six months before I could test her blood myself. I knew it was the only way to know what was going on with her at all times. I was not going to give up, because going to the vet's constantly was too emotional for both of us.

It was becoming increasingly difficult to get Lucy's blood sugar under control, so more tests were ordered only to find out she had Cushing's disease—a disorder that occurs when a person or dog's body is exposed to high levels of the hormone cortisol—as well. Only 10 percent of dogs have both diabetes and Cushing's. Lucy had every doctor imaginable to help her, including Dr. Kevin Cummins, who was there with us every step of the way; a wonderful eye doctor who restored her sight, which had been lost to the diabetes; an endocrinologist in New York City; and even an acupuncturist, who was my last resort in helping Lucy.

I purchased a doggie stroller for Lucy, since she loved going on walks; with the stroller we could go on longer ones, and she could still enjoy the fresh air. Lillian used to meet us every day, and once a week she would buy Lucy's favorite squeaker toy—because Lucy expected a new one *every week*. She would start barking and carrying on at the first sight of Lillian.

My life was consumed with trying to halt these diseases, but after almost three years they finally claimed Lucy's life. They were too much for her little body, and she died at home, in my arms, at ten years of age.

Tears fill my eyes as I write this because the void in my life is so big—one that can never be filled. As I listen to "I Will Survive," I know I will survive, and that somehow, somewhere, I'll gather the strength not to fall apart—but boy, oh boy, did I love Lucy.

ANGELS IN THE ASHES

by Bobbie Cole

When "I Will Survive" debuted, I was newly divorced and a public-school music teacher. My kids loved the song, so now and then I'd have it playing on the stereo as they entered the music building. There was nothing like an upbeat, empowering tune to put them in the mood for an hour of music, especially if their class before mine had been a downer. It didn't hurt for their instructor to feel positive either.

Years later, I was caught up in a tragedy beyond imagination—as a first responder at the Oklahoma City bombing in 1995. My then eighteen-year-old son was with me. We escaped the explosion but stayed to see what we could do. It was easier to think than to feel, because our city had been violated, ripped apart, and cool heads and helping hands were needed in hundreds of capacities to restore order and repair damage.

The first thing we did was don the required OSHA gear and sit on a curb with the small number of others who were first responders. We waited nearly an hour before hearing the disturbing news: Aside from the walking wounded who were outside when the blast occurred, few, if any, survivors were visible within the destroyed building. Hushed murmurs of *oh no* swept through our small group. We braced ourselves, never imagining the horrors we would soon come to see. Then we received our assignments.

Since my son was big, strong, and willing, and since he had a bit of medical training, he was sent to ground zero to help set up a triage unit, to aid any survivors, and to excavate victim remains. A nurse and I set up the county sheriff's command post four blocks north of ground zero.

Our morning started with a warm spring sun and no shade. There also weren't any tables for the triage. A young man, a representative with Sonic Corporation, was the first to show up and ask what we needed. My requests were for toilet paper, latrines, coffee, and food. Within an hour or so more help came, and sheriffs from all over the state arrived—some on horseback, because ground zero was in shambles and no cars could get through. During the first hour or so, the only people on the streets were first responders.

Someone delivered tents and tables. Local law enforcement set perimeters, and the process of establishing order was transferred smoothly from state to federal administration. With every truckload of food and beverages, and with the arrival of every firefighter, police officer, and armed guard, my heart sank as I thought of the jobs they'd have to do.

Our group of responders was joined by hysterical mothers and fathers. They descended upon us, demanding to be taken to the bomb site, shaking with sobs and screaming for their babies in the day-care center. Until then, my mind had compartmentalized everything, reducing the unfolding drama to facts, without feeling. A bomb had blown up a building filled with people. That's what I needed to concentrate on. But those people had relatives, friends, spouses, children . . . and when the tears and screams were in my face, cold facts gave way to shaky emotion. I'd volunteered, but now I doubted my ability to help.

Eventually, our headquarters buzzed with the sounds of somber voices and crackling walkie-talkies. More food arrived, along with batteries, raincoats, and flashlights from Walmart. By that time, a foreboding, overcast sky darkened the area.

Reporters were for the most part respectful and didn't press the issue when they were refused admittance. As word of the bombing hit the airwaves, more horrified parents arrived, screaming for their children. Police officers had the difficult task of restraining and comforting them. Clergy arrived, as did more doctors and nurses. The sky opened and the rain began.

My son and I were there from 9:15 A.M. until one something the next morning—eighteen hours, most of it in the pouring rain. Much of it for me was spent ordering supplies for firemen, police officers, and, eventually, the Oklahoma National Guard and FEMA.

At some point that afternoon, when rain was replaced with a cold drizzle, one of the sheriffs suggested I take a break. There was still much to do, so I hopped onto the bed of a pickup and rode slowly through the sea of rescuers, stopping every few feet to dispense hot coffee, bottled water, sandwiches, flashlights, and batteries.

I didn't realize until I jumped out of the truck to stretch my legs that we were at the bomb site. Until then, I'd concentrated on keeping an encouraging smile on my face, eyes lowered or making contact with workers—just to offer support and let them know they weren't alone. I hadn't surveyed my surroundings.

Now . . . *I was horrified.* The scene resembled photos I'd seen of Beirut. Debris, body parts, the ground thick with shards of glass, splintered wood, pieces of timber, huge blocks of cement, gray ashes, torn clothing, and crayon drawings done by the children at the day-care center.

I wobbled on shaky legs—almost losing my balance—and leaned against a fireman, who caught me. Righting myself, I tried focusing on anything that would keep me steady. One solitary sight grabbed my attention: a toddler's once-white shoe, now soot covered, lodged like some bizarre modern-art sculpture between two massive concrete boulders. A creaking sound alarmed me. I looked up and saw a thin cable holding one of the cement slabs trapping the shoe. My gaze traveled vertically, then horizontally, and eventually back to the shoe.

Sweet Lord . . . I was at ground zero, standing where the day-care center had been. Only a few hours earlier, fifteen children and their caregivers had perished there.

Remnants of the Murrah Federal Building groaned in the breeze as wires and cables held tons of weight that could collapse at any moment. Yet no one seemed intent on fleeing. In danger or not, I wasn't leaving either. I knew in an instant that what I felt resonated with every worker at the site. We were connected by commitment. There was no choice as far as we were concerned. Our jobs had to be done. We would stay as long as was necessary.

My first reaction was to murmur the Lord's Prayer. My body shook. I couldn't conceive of the hatred and lack of compassion that could cause an act like this. I could barely remember the words, even though I'd recited them hundreds of times over the years. Granted, previously my head had always been bowed. Now I whispered the words while viewing an ocean of destruction and thousands of people—some moving with determination, others adrift, performing their jobs by rote. Their faces haunted me. Their eyes spoke volumes of pain and disbelief.

My second reaction was to calm my racing heart and shattered nerves, to pause and consciously see, to remove the focus from my own fears and take note of the angels among the ashes. They were firemen, policemen, and members of churches and businesses who freely contributed their time and money to pull the community together. Even a homeless man pushed a cart of grilled-cheese sandwiches made by helping hands. Firemen coming from the bowels of the crumbled building passed me, their grimy faces smeared with tears and sweat. I cried, sharing their pain, imagining the horrors they had encountered.

I thought of my son, who had been with one of the first crews to enter the site. He was a young man, but he was my child, and I knew he bore witness to death and devastation no one should see. I hadn't encountered him for hours and wondered how he was, if he was safe, and how he would cope in the aftermath. The only thing I could do was trust a power greater than any of us to watch over him.

Shock would set in if I didn't focus on something. It was then that I started humming softly, the first thing that entered my mind— Gloria Gaynor's tune, only it wasn't lively. It was slow—more like a dirge—as if I had slowed my mind to really consider the meaning of the lyrics.

A montage of emotions washed through me. Gratitude for having escaped with my life and good health. Sorrow for the families and friends who had lost loved ones . . . sons, daughters, mothers, fathers. It was no wonder, I'd reflect later, that so many responders would take their own lives on the anniversary of the bombing. The grief and trauma were overwhelming.

Before leaving for home that evening, I had seen strong men crying, cadaver dogs trembling with exhaustion, blood-soaked nurses continuing to work, and the traumatized, hollow-eyed families of the victims. I had also seen great compassion, empathy, and amazing acts of kindness.

One of the county sheriffs left around 11:00 P.M., and I knew where he had parked. It would take him several minutes to reach his vehicle in the blinding rain. Yet he took off his rain gear and told me to keep it. "Give it to the next guy who shows up to work and doesn't have a coat."

I didn't cry for several days, because I couldn't allow myself the luxury. So many men and women had depended upon my ability to take care of their needs while they handled the unthinkable tasks of rescue, recovery, identifying the remains, and cleaning up the devastation. Months later, I suffered survivor's guilt. There were 169 souls who didn't make it, including a pretty nurse who had been near me as we waited for our assignments. That one of the rescuers could die hadn't occurred to me while we were there. I didn't know what to do with that, how to unload what I'd seen and heard. I didn't know how to handle the sadness. So I bottled my feelings.

As I had expected, my son too was unable to talk about his experiences at length. We stuck to familiar, mundane chores and light conversation for months following that day. Then, years later, he came to me smiling and said he had something for me to hear. It was the band Cake, performing their cover version of "I Will Survive."

I smiled my appreciation and patted his arm. "Thanks."

Nearly two decades later, I still try to make sense of that day in April. It began with such promise, bright sunshine, and laughter. By afternoon it was beyond dismal. By evening, the day's events had tested me like I'd never been tested before. I was numb. So much devastation, so many lives lost, and innumerable broken hearts left to mourn them.

I'd always heard that in order to help others we should first check our own pulse. "I Will Survive" helped me check mine. I've bumped booties with friends while listening to the song, played it for students, and quietly reflected on its lyrics at a time when it was my rock, my strength, and a subtle yet constant promise of better days to come.

WHEN A CHILD DIES
by Sandy Fox

W hen the phone rang at 11:30 P.M. on March 2, 1994, I was awoken from a sound sleep. I was told my daughter, Marcy, had been killed that night in a car accident on her way home from work, after she and her husband, Simon, had picked up their new car. It was a horrific accident: A man going seventy miles an hour in a residential area plowed into the side of their car after running a stop sign on a busy Los Angeles street. My daughter and son-in-law's car was thrown against a tree, flipping over and over. Marcy died instantly. Simon eventually recovered to a degree he could live with after fifteen years of surgeries and treatments. The driver was never caught, even though a large reward was offered.

Not surprisingly, it still seems like just yesterday. My mind thinks it has not been that long since I last saw Marcy. Time has a way of distorting our lives, particularly when something so traumatic happens.

I remember screaming and screaming that night, unable and unwilling to accept what had happened. *What a waste, what a waste,* I kept saying, *of a wonderful child, the wonderful life she had, all the plans she'd made . . . all the plans I had made with her. This happens to other people, not me. I'm a good person. What had I done to deserve this? Why? Why? Why?* There were so many questions and no answers.

Marcy was my only child. She was a beautiful twenty-seven-year-old woman—bright, energetic, enthusiastic, caring, considerate . . . There are not enough adjectives to describe her. I realize most parents would say the same of their children, but it was all validated for me after her death when I received hundreds of letters and notes from her friends and co-workers, who told me how "she was the glue that held people together; at any expense, she was helpful and kind to anyone who needed her." I didn't know others felt that way, and it has always warmed my heart to know they have confirmed what I also felt.

For months I didn't care about anything. I simply didn't know what to do and, particularly, how to feel. I knew that I couldn't go on this way, not eating right, not taking care of myself or doing the things I needed to do. Some friends sent books for me to read, and that became a great help. I read them all and realized that what I was feeling was normal. I was not crazy.

Those first years were hard. My future was gone. Everything I had hoped for my daughter—a career, a family, to enjoy life, to travel—were gone in a split second. How would I survive this devastation? Teaching helped. It filled my days so I couldn't think of my loss. I'd come home and find cards from friends of mine and friends of Marcy's. One day I came home to find nothing in my mailbox and cried my heart out. They were going to forget her. They were moving on with their own lives. Now what?

Friends and relatives helped by inviting my husband and me to dinner or to go out for another type of distraction. After a time that came more easily, and I found I could laugh again without feeling guilty that I was alive and Marcy wasn't. Hearing music that my daughter loved helped. Gloria Gaynor's song "I Will Survive" became my motto. Although not all the lyrics applied to my situation, the determination of the woman singing those lines inspired me to want to make the best of my life, to love others unconditionally, to live every day to the fullest after experiencing the worst thing that could ever happen to a parent. I knew by then I was moving forward.

There are some parents who want to just lie down at night and never wake up again. I was not like that. I didn't know it at first, but I had a different calling. I knew I wanted to live and to do something useful, something that would make Marcy proud of me and that I could make her part of. I needed to make a difference. And if I could help just one person, that would be enough. I set out on that goal. All bereaved parents should try to find something they are interested in to make their lives meaningful again. That is such a big help as one travels through the never-ending journey of grief.

I was not young enough to have additional children, but I could certainly help people in a variety of ways. First I had to tell others about my own feelings so they could identify with me. I then realized that other stories would also help define us and show bereaved parents they could move on with their lives in a positive direction. Since I had been a journalist my whole life, I knew that writing all this down might help others in similar circumstances and, in turn, provide a catharsis for myself as well. Hence, I published my first book on surviving the death of a child, *I Have No Intention of Saying Good-bye*. The book was well received, partly because there was not much else out there at the time to help struggling parents. I received many notes of thanks for my words of comfort and still do so to this day. There is nothing that pleases me more than receiving thanks from bereaved parents.

I also began speaking at national bereavement conferences and to a variety of groups around the country, meeting parents, hearing about their losses and what they were feeling. I made many new friends and kept thinking of Marcy, and how both of us were helping others in a way I had never dreamed of. Marcy had always kidded me about writing the great American novel, but never in my wildest imagination did I think my first book would feature her in the center. My will to survive—born out of my longing to keep my daughter's memory alive, as well as the song "I Will Survive"—kept me going and encouraged me to continue my work.

Ten years later, I felt a desire to let other bereaved parents know how to survive after the initial grieving period was over. "What now?" some asked me. "What can I do to honor my child and keep her memory alive?" What should you do if you're feeling stuck in a particular situation, dealing with marital problems, or just want to know how others manage their feelings of guilt? These questions and others produced my second book, *Creating a New Normal . . . After the Death of a Child.*

Six years ago I started a bereavement group in Scottsdale, Arizona, where I live, specifically for parents who have lost either their only child or all their children. We come together every other month, have a program dealing with our childless situations, and just talk and have fun. There is laughter in our group and sometimes tears, but we all understand how the others are feeling and try to help one another. I have watched all of the members grow and survive their personal ordeals and am very proud of them. I stay not because I need to be in a group anymore, but because I love them all and want to remain in touch.

I have found many ways to honor Marcy, both from my new friends and from reading lots of books on grief. The one thing bereaved parents want more than anything else is to make sure their child is not forgotten, and there are many ways to do this: through scholarships, foundations, buying bricks, dedicating buildings or plaques in various locations, or simply talking about their losses to anyone who will listen.

I have a new life with new goals and new priorities, and I'm loving it. My second husband and I travel frequently, and each place we go, we make sure Marcy is with us, if only in spirit. At every new location, I say to him, "Marcy would have loved seeing this." They never got to meet, but I know she would have loved him as much as I do. He feels her presence all the time and talks about her emotionally to others as if she were his own. I try to leave something of hers when we travel or place a special rock in an area and then go into a church or synagogue and light a candle for her. She is in my thoughts and actions every day. Even though a part of my heart was cut out when she died, I can feel her with me wherever I am. I sometimes believe I am living the life she would have led and doing things for others that she would have done. It is comforting, and I will continue to survive knowing she is always by my side.

I LIVED TO SING AGAIN

by Maria Judge

I planned my funeral the Christmas I was twenty-seven.

Earlier that month I'd found a lump in my breast, and in the two weeks it took to have a mammogram, wait for the results to come back, and get an appointment with a doctor, I assumed the worst. Convinced I had cancer and anticipating my certain death, I planned for my eventual demise. I envisioned my whole family participating in the funeral Mass, to be held at the parish church in my hometown and concelebrated by several of our family's priestly friends. Mom and Dad would do the readings, my sisters would play the piano and flute during the service, and my brother would play taps on his trumpet at the cemetery. I was still pondering the choice of a eulogist—one of my other five siblings, perhaps a longtime friend—when I finally got in to see the doctor. He stuck a needle in the lump, pronounced it a cyst, drained the fluid, and sent me on my way. I called off the embalmers and canceled the clerics.

Fifteen Decembers later, I found another lump. Again it was a cyst and again a surgeon aspirated it. It disappeared but came back a few weeks later. I thought it looked the same. So did the ultrasound technician. So did the surgeon. We weren't worried. He didn't think cancer, I didn't think cancer; no one thought cancer, no one said cancer.

Except for the pathologist. He found cancer in the tissue around the cyst. We didn't know how much was there, how far it had spread, or anything else about it. Just that it was cancer.

A few more rounds of testing determined I would need a year's worth of treatment—surgery, chemo, and radiation—some of which had side effects that seemed almost as bad as the cancer itself. As the oncologist described these procedures, a background commentary ran through my head.

She explained the chemo's effect on my bone marrow: the toxic drugs killed off the good cells along with the bad and, when the white cells were low, the immune system was suppressed, so I should stay away from sick people when I was at the low point of the cycle. (*How could I avoid sick people when I'd be spending the next year in hospitals and oncology centers?*) There was often nausea and vomiting (*nine months with my head in the toilet*), hair loss (*good thing I look OK with short hair*), and fatigue (*I'm already an insomniac, so I should be completely sleepless after this*).

Chemo could weaken the heart muscle and cause irregular or rapid rhythms (*I already have an irregular heartbeat; it'll be going triple time after this!*), and irritate the tissue if it gets outside the veins (*good thing I have great veins*). It also causes mouth sores and diarrhea (*nine months of diarrhea? I'll have it coming out of both ends*), irritates the bladder, so I'd need to drink a lot of water (*OK, now we've got nausea, diarrhea, and peeing—I'm going to need three toilets*), can cause premature menopause (*hot flashes during nausea*), and put you at risk of developing another cancer (*no witty comeback for this one, the prospect just terrified me*).

I called my sister when I got home. "You're bigger than this," she reminded me. "You'll beat it. You're a survivor." I kept reminding myself of that. *I'll survive this. I will!*

Each of my twelve chemotherapy sessions would last about two hours, and all I had to do was sit in the chair and wait while the poison dripped into my vein. Each infusion room had a television, so I could use that to distract myself during the sessions. I doubted I could concentrate on a television show and thought I'd be better off relaxing and letting everything around me fade away. Music could help me to do that.

I'd grown up with music in my life. My parents sang around the house, my siblings and I took music lessons and played instruments (some more successfully than others), and I sang in high school, college musicals, and community and church choirs. I always appreciated music's ability to move and motivate me, as well as to connect me to the time and place where I'd first heard a song. It seemed a very useful tool to have with me in an infusion room. So I went through my collection of records, tapes, and CDs to assemble an assortment of humorous and healing songs that I thought would give me the boost I would need during my long and challenging treatment program. I recorded everything onto a tape—this was 1997, before MP3 players and iTunes—and packed my cassette player in the bag I took with me to treatment. Every few weeks for the next year, Gloria Gaynor reminded me that I would survive. Of course, I added my background commentary here too:

At first, I was afraid, I was petrified, she sang. I could relate to that.

And then, *I grew strong!* I did.

I learned how to get along! Chemo sessions quickly became routine and just fit into my daily routine.

Just turn around now, 'Cause you're not welcome anymore. I pictured the cancer being turned away and escorted down the hall to the trash.

Did you think I'd crumble, Did you think I'd lay down and die? Oh, no, not I! I went back to work, made people laugh, and kept up with most things I wanted to do.

I hold my head up high. My bald, beautiful, slightly immune-suppressed head.

Go on now. That's pretty much what I did. I just went on.

It helped that I didn't have many of the side effects I'd feared. I did pee a lot and got fatigued. My hair fell out, but not as soon as they predicted, and it grew back quickly. I never got nauseous, didn't have diarrhea, no mouth sores ever materialized, my heart beat steadily but not too fast, and sixteen years later I'm still cancer free. But the music in the infusion room also helped on all fronts, relaxing me, reminding me of other places and better times, and helping me focus on positives—on life and living and survival.

Still, it wasn't an easy year. My father, aunt, and uncle were diagnosed with cancer around the same time as I was, and Dad died ten weeks after his diagnosis. A work colleague, a friend, and two other friends' mothers also died of cancer that year. Three other friends and six more relatives were diagnosed a few years later. There were times when I felt surrounded by the disease. Some days I thought I would need to play the song all day long, just to remind myself I was going to get through this. It always helped.

Over the years I've shared the song with friends facing illness, injury, or the loss of too many loved ones. The message even cheered up my whole office a few years ago when a colleague required emergency surgery. I bought her a musical get-well card that played "I Will Survive" and left it at the front desk for people to sign. Every time someone opened it, the song could be heard throughout the entire floor. We were in hysterics by the end of the day.

Last week two bombs exploded near the finish line of the Boston Marathon, just a few blocks from my office. Three people were killed and more than two hundred injured; many of the survivors lost limbs. We continue to hear stories of the strength shown by the injured, the courage of those who rushed to help them, and the generosity of the donors who have raised millions of dollars to help. Music fills the background of many of the stories: songs of inspiration, motivation, and strength for the difficult journey that lies ahead. And one of the songs I heard was "I Will Survive."

As I walk by the memorials in Copley Plaza each day on my way to and from work, I softly sing, "You will survive."

BOUNTIFUL HARVEST

by Cathi LaMarche

During a dinner party with friends and acquaintances, the topic of collectors' items arose, and lively chatter ensued. The women waxed sentimental while recalling their childhood memorabilia in keepsake boxes stowed inside closets and underneath beds. Whenever nostalgia took hold, they said they would sift through the trinkets and treasures to loosen the memories lodged in dark crevices, allowing a journey back to simpler days filled with a mother's love and a father's embrace.

"The best years of my life are stashed away in that box," one woman said. "What I wouldn't give to be a kid again."

I remained silent, as I often did when talk of younger years surfaced. Not all childhoods are worthy of veneration. One of the women noticed my reserve and pulled me into the conversation. "So, Cathi, what did you collect as a child?" She smiled, eagerly awaiting my answer.

Did she really want to know? A couple of her friends leaned in with eyes wide as I fought the urge to take the easier path and lie. After all, I had become an expert liar in years past whenever prying eyes stared at a fresh cut on my lip. A purplish imprint of fingers across my forearm, or myriad bug bites on my body after having been locked out of my family home by my mother. And there was my lie in response to the doctor's probing question as to why I had an ulcer at ten, a truth that was better left untold for fear the violence would escalate. Besides, would he even believe that, as I nestled in bed at night, my mother threatened to harm me while I slept? Ironically, I soon viewed anyone who asked me questions out of concern for my well-being as a potential threat to my safety, so the words "everything is fine" and "it was just an accident" became my mantras.

This evening the urge to reject honesty remained strong as I sat under the women's scrutiny. Perhaps I should tell them I'd collected miniature glass horses, handblown and colorful, like the ones I admired in the dime-store window, or the Chinese nesting dolls I had longed to crawl inside to protect myself each night from the yelling, the name calling, and the punching. No, I had to tell the truth—that what I had collected couldn't be tucked inside a souvenir box. And it certainly wasn't something to cherish.

The women continued to wait for my answer, and the room suddenly felt smaller, the air stifling. I needed courage to speak out, so I summoned Gloria Gaynor's song to inspire me, as it had so many times in the past.

Did you think I'd crumble?

Did you think I'd lay down and die?

I hadn't crumbled as a child, and I wouldn't crumble now. Speaking for all the children who had suffered at the hands of an adult, I drew a breath and said, "Bruises." I sipped my coffee. "I collected bruises. All shapes and sizes, really."

A couple of ladies shifted in their chairs. There was the clank of a spoon, a whisper, followed by silence. The smiles faded. The topic changed abruptly. No one dared to ask a follow-up question. Could I blame them? Obviously, I had taken them by surprise.

Regret suddenly surfaced. Divulging intimate information always carried risk and, after all these years, shame still lurked about it. Maybe it was having to admit that my mother didn't love me and had left without as much as a good-bye. Maybe it was the morbid curiosity of those who asked if it was physical, sexual, or emotional abuse I had suffered—as if to rate my trauma on their scale of injustice. Maybe it was the fear that people would think I somehow deserved it after noting my character flaws. After all, who wants to believe that such a travesty happens to innocent children?

Awkwardness settled in for the evening and conversation came in spurts, all superficial, as if to avoid potentially digging into anyone's past for fear of what else might be unearthed. Every so often I would spy someone gazing at me, perhaps searching for lasting marks. To look at me, you'd never guess that I was a product of such dysfunction. As a proud mother, wife, award-winning educator, author, and friend, I didn't show any lasting scars—ones they could see, anyway. They saw a happily married woman with a well-adjusted family and a successful career. But it wasn't always so.

I used to cry but now I hold my head up high.

And you see me, somebody new . . .

It had taken me years to realize that the abuse I suffered as a child could benefit me as an adult. In my teens and early twenties the pain was too raw, too fresh to reconcile. In my attempts to escape the gut-wrenching memories, I succumbed to self-destructive behaviors, taking an easier path paved with vices, blame, and denial. Embarrassed by neighborhood gossip, unsightly bruises, and the red-and-blue swirl of police cars in the driveway, I prayed for a different home, a different family, a different me.

It took all the strength I had not to fall apart . . .

After the diagnosis of an autoimmune disorder, followed by the unraveling of my first marriage, I finally invited self-acceptance into my life. Soon I realized that I had collected more than bruises along the way; I held a treasure trove of rich details and experiences, providing strength and an impetus for positive changes in my life. My childhood treks in the woods, lasting for hours on end until dusk forced me home, gifted me with an appreciation for the value of silence and the art of self-reflection, a respect and an admiration for the earth's natural beauty, and the moxie to become self-sufficient. This bountiful harvest of painful life lessons propelled me forward, allowing me to overcome each new setback.

And I grew strong and I learned how to get along . . .

These days I'm rewarded when watching my son and daughter revel in childhood adventures. They remain inquisitive and intrigued by nature's offerings, absorbing the wonders around them as beneficiaries of the knowledge I obtained throughout those tumultuous childhood years. In the stillness of the woods, our family delights in a wide-eyed doe with her wobbly-legged fawn whose ears twitch at the crunching of leaves beneath our feet; the three-syllable call of a covey of bobwhite quail strutting across an old, dirt path; the rush of a stream filled with the melted snow of winter's fury. My children have learned to respect and admire the world's simplicity and splendor through my eyes, the same eyes that once canvassed the outdoors for shelter and solace from abusive hands. Now we luxuriate over such natural beauty that others fail to notice, and my past completes our present.

But despite my recent successes, I have never dismissed my past. Discounting the remnants of sadness—as though the abuse never occurred—would belittle all I learned from my years of misfortune. To this day I still gravitate toward hard-luck newspaper articles, sorrowful movies, and four-hankie novels because they're familiar, even comfortable at times. When immersed in the world of the downtrodden, my past worms its way into the present and the distinctive lines separating my life from others' softens, resulting in an abundance of compassion for people I have never met. Yet another gift. And, while I offer empathy to those in need, I certainly don't pity the people whose tragedies outnumber their good fortunes, because adversity begets fortitude—another blessing I have come to appreciate.

To say that I've reached the apex of happiness would be an overstatement; rather, I've reached a state of symbiosis where my childhood, enveloped in sadness, and my current life, enwrapped with the love of my husband and children, do not compete for attention but amicably share space. Intricately woven together—a web of life experiences—they offer hope for continued blessings yet remind me that other hardships will undoubtedly surface. Because of this bountiful harvest of life's teachings, I possess the mettle to meet such challenges.

I will survive.

GUKURAHUNDI

by Tendai Mwanaka

O ver 20,000 died and the mounting death toll kept mounting . . .
I was a little boy of about seven. I was at the kraals (a tradi-
tional African village of huts), about to take the goats and cattle to the
graze lands, when I saw the PUMA Army vehicles coming into our
village. I knew it meant trouble. Recently, the fearsome Fifth Brigade
had been deployed in our area. We had heard news about them from
the other villages of Filabusi. They hadn't been to our village before.
Our village was a quiet one. But in all the villages the brigade had
been to, only a few had survived to tell the story. They were said to be
wiping out whole villages. *Gukurahundi* simply meant "the wiping
out of whole villages."

When I saw those PUMA Army vehicles and the soldiers, I took
cover in the gully near our kraals. It was simply a survival instinct.
I watched as they collected the whole village, as if we were nothing
but dried cow dung (*hundi* in *Gukurahundi*) for burning. It wasn't
difficult to do because our village was close-knit, almost a high-den-
sity suburb. They took everyone to just beyond our cattle kraals, near
the village burial site. They took my father, my mom, and my two
little sisters as well. I was petrified but couldn't tear myself away. I
followed close behind but still undercover.

It was in 1985, about October. Our leaders—Joshua Nkomo,
Ndumiso Dabengwa—and others had been waging a recalcitrant war
against Robert Mugabe's alienation policies on the Ndebele people
for nearly two years. During that time we hadn't seen or been caught
in the crossfire until about two weeks before that fateful day, when

they had started ransacking our Filabusi area. Up until then the war had been concentrated in the Matabeleland north province, in the Lupane area. There were many rebels there. Most of the political leaders of the ZAPU party—the mother body of the ZIPRA rebels who had been waging this war—also came from Matabeleland, just north of our region.

At the grave sites, they accused the villagers of protecting Gwesira and the rebels who were fighting this civil war. The villagers denied the allegation, saying that they had neither seen nor fed any rebels. But this argument didn't last long. The notorious Fifth Brigade shot a couple of people to show they meant business. They told the villagers to start digging a huge hole for their burial. Nobody in his right mind would have gone against this command.

I watched as the people started digging their own graves using their hands, sometimes with nothing more than sticks or stones to help them. I saw my family among them. I could see the terror on their faces and the blood on their hands. I was seething with anger, trembling with fear, and dying with grief inside, wanting to do something to stop them but helpless to do anything. Those soldiers watched, unmoved in the face of this inhumanity.

Ours was a sizable village of over thirty households. At the grave site, nearly two hundred of my closest relations cowered together against the fifteen armed-to-the-teeth soldiers. There was nothing they could have done. There was nothing I could have done. I couldn't get out of my hiding place because it meant instant death. I watched for over three hours as my friends and family dug a hole deep enough and big enough to accommodate the entire village.

Sometime in the midafternoon, the soldiers told the villagers to stand by the mouth of the grave, five at a time. Five soldiers stood there as well. I heard them as they asked the villagers to tell them where the rebels were. I heard them warn my people that if they kept quiet, they would shoot them and they would fall into the grave. They were clear that they would shoot anyone who lied. We all knew that even if we told the truth, there was only one end to this moment. Each would collapse into the grave, life after life wasted.

The other ten soldiers were securing and guarding the place. It was difficult to keep track of the killing. I simply died inside watching, but I still watched. That afternoon, the soldiers wiped out the whole village and pushed everyone into the grave—even those who were still alive, including the village's helpless, innocent children. I was the only one saved.

I don't remember seeing them kill my family, but I know they were killed. No one escaped. Once every person was inside the grave, the soldiers took the shovels from their PUMA Army trucks and started covering the grave with soil and stones. Some people were buried alive. It took them several hours to bury my village, but I didn't wait or watch. I couldn't stand it anymore. I walked to the next village, and the next, and the next, while the soldiers were still there. I drifted southward with the wind. I kept walking for days on end, eating whatever I could get from the bushes or from other villages. I just wanted to get as far away as possible from those killing fields.

How I survived I don't know. I know only that I survived. Many villages other than ours were also cleansed during those years. Many people were buried alive in mass graves in the Matabeleland region.

I grew up in Gwanda town, adopted by a childless family there. I told them my name was Sibusiso. They adopted everything except my heart, which had died that October day. My heart had fallen, buried into the earth, along with my village.

But one day I was listening to the song by Gloria Gaynor, "I Will Survive," on Jacaranda FM, a Gauteng, South Africa, radio station, especially these lyrics . . . *Oh, no, not I, I will survive, oh as long as I know how to love I know I'll stay alive. I've got all my life to live, I've got all my love to give and I'll survive, I will survive.* So I thought maybe with these loving people, I can learn how to love again and really survive.

These lyrics would often come back to my mind, and I would be humming them and thinking of how Gloria must have survived a very difficult relationship back then. After remembering these lyrics recently and, hearing of her book, I was inspired to write my story. It happened a long time ago, and I had buried the memories deep down inside.

I knew that writing would give me an opportunity to go back to it, to relive the events, but keeping the song's lyrics in my mind through the process has inspired me to truly survive.

HENRY'S DIAGNOSIS

by Sarah Heffernan

In the summer of 2008, my twin boys went to a golf camp in Dorchester, Massachusetts, for a week. There I met a neighbor of mine, Cindy, who lives about twenty houses down the street from me. We talked every day during our sons' golf lessons, and I found her to be fascinating because we talked mostly about her son, Sam, who has Type 1 diabetes—formerly known as juvenile diabetes. I found her knowledge about the disease, and how well the family controlled it, truly impressive.

In August 2009 I had flashbacks to my talks with Cindy. I remembered her telling me what signs to look out for and actually playfully laughing at me because I am a hypochondriac and thought *all* my three kids had diabetes—if not Type 1, then Type 2.

To this day, I remember going to a mall to do some back-to-school shopping. My children and I went to Target, and my son Henry, aged nine, asked me if I could buy him some bottled water. I said, "No, go drink from the water fountain." So he and his twin, Kirby, ran over to the fountain, and then they quickly had to use the restroom. Next up was Best Buy. Again, Henry asked if I could get him bottled water. He was driving me crazy, but for some reason I kept thinking of Cindy saying "always thirsty . . . can't quench his thirst." Then we went to Office Max and, once again, Henry asked me if I could buy him more bottled water and if he could use the restroom. I remembered Cindy saying, "Going to the bathroom more than normal is a sign."

From that day I watched Henry like a hawk. I would stay up at night and think it was Kirby, his twin, going to the bathroom and then Henry going to the bathroom—but no, it was Henry, Henry, Henry.

In September, Henry had a swim party and, as he put on his bathing suit, I could see every rib in his back. Now you have to know my family. We eat ribs; we don't *show* ribs. I was shocked. Again Cindy's words came into my head: "unexpected weight loss." When Henry started the fourth grade, I knew his teacher very well, and I made a comment to him: "You know what, I might be crazy, but I think Henry has diabetes. I'm going to get him checked out."

On Thursday, September 24, I confirmed my kids' flu shots for the following Monday. I said to the nurse, "Oh, Pat, do you think you could check Henry for diabetes? I think he has it." She was absolutely floored and really not quite sure what to say to me. She said, "Sarah, oh my lord, if you really think he has it, you have to bring him in now." Since it was Thursday and I was heading to New York City for the weekend, I figured I could wait until Monday. Still, that whole weekend, I prayed I was only being neurotic.

Soon enough, it was Monday, September 28. We went to the doctor's office at 4:00 P.M., but the doctor was running late. It wasn't until after 5:00 P.M. when we were finally called in. I said I would like Henry to be checked for diabetes. I felt like I was going to faint. The thought of him being diagnosed would kill pieces of my heart, plus make me feel guilty that I had taken so long to get him checked.

That's when our little world crumbled. The nurse, who had known Henry and Kirby since they were three days old, came over to me and hugged me as she said, "He does. He's going to be OK, but he has Type 1 diabetes." Right behind her was Henry's pediatrician, and even he hugged me and said, "I am so sorry." That's when I wanted to cry, but I tried with all my might to keep it together for Henry. Within seconds a team of doctors and nurses from endocrinology were all over my son. They were so good and caring about what was going on. I had called my husband, Walter, and he came right in, and we got a crash course about Type 1 diabetes. It was amazing to me, because I clearly had picked up on all the symptoms from Cindy's conversation, but I hadn't really soaked in what diabetes was. All I wanted from the doctors now was to hear that Henry was going to be fine.

The first year was hard for all of us. I called 911 when Henry's numbers were low . . . I called them when they were off the chart . . . After coming to our house, the EMS workers assured me he'd be OK. Henry had to have shots of insulin given to him by Walter or me, and then there was our new world of carb counting.

One Thanksgiving I remember looking over at the kids' table and seeing Henry eating his food alone, the last kid left at the table. Yes, all of his food had been noted on a chart, but I wondered what he was thinking. How would juvenile diabetes, which ironically lasts a lifetime, impact his future? God, tears just rolled down my face. I thought, *we can get through this, but how?*

It was also scary for us to have him leave our side. My husband and I wanted Henry next to us for the rest of his life, and we didn't want anyone or anything to interfere with him and his treatment. Cindy had mentioned to me that I should sign Henry up for diabetes camp. She told me it was a wonderful camp for kids and teenagers with Type 1 diabetes run by the Joslin Diabetes Center. She said it was a *must* that he go, and that he would love it. This would be Henry's first time away from us and, because he was newly diagnosed with the disease, I was hesitant to send him. But I did. It took all my strength not to fall apart. I went through hell the first week he was there. First I kept thinking, *are they going to really know what to do with him and his diabetes?* Parents could go online and look at camp pictures—and yes, these were candid shots—but Henry was *never* smiling, so I knew something was wrong. The camp prefers parents not to call, but, well, I couldn't help myself. I called repeatedly. Finally I talked with Henry's head counselor, and she told me he was having a ball. She said, "He is a really funny kid, and he makes friends really easily. He is having a great time."

I broke down and cried. It was like hearing that I'd won the lottery. I was so happy to hear that Henry was living a "normal" and fun life! Then I talked with Cindy, and she assured me, "It's a camp just for diabetics. They know what they are doing. In fact, the counselors are diabetics, the nurses are diabetics, the doctors . . . it's their one happy world!" When we picked Henry up after two weeks (20,160 minutes, to be exact!), he said it was the best two weeks of his life!

It's been four years and Henry now relies on a pump, or the OmniPod, to give him his insulin. My husband and I no longer have to deal with giving him his shots. Henry wants nothing to do with us anymore and likes to be at his friends' houses, or at summer camp— not just Camp Joslin, but ones for golf and baseball too. He loves playing sports and drinking his "bottled" water. He even goes away on overnights, and it's gotten to the point where I can now sleep without worrying about him.

Henry takes excellent care of his diabetes, and we are so proud to be his parents as he turns thirteen next week. I actually like being a parent with a child who has diabetes. I think it helps us all balance the important things in life. It also reminds me of a song I dance to all the time with a fake microphone, under a little disco ball I have in the kitchen of my house. "Henry," I always say, like I'm a disco queen, "this song's for you: 'I Will Survive'!" And then I just move to the beat, knowing that we have survived, all thanks to Gloria Gaynor and my talks with Cindy.

I'LL BE THERE

by Andrea Walker

Y ou have breast cancer. I'm sorry about that."
The doctor's words make my head spin. She looks down, avoiding my eyes. I catch my breath. My husband, Bob, who is seated next to me, puts his arm around my shoulder.

"How did this happen?" I whisper to the doctor. "I'm not behind on my mammograms. There's no history of cancer in my family."

Numb, I am unaware of her reply. Somehow those factors don't matter. She goes on to describe stage 2 and the protocol. Do I have a surgeon I want to use for the lumpectomy? "No?" She can recommend one. Ten minutes tick by while she calls the surgeon's office and sets up a consultation. Two weeks. Every step in the process of diagnosis has happened in week-long increments. Now I will live with this evil invasion another two weeks before I can see a surgeon who will cut it out.

Survival enters my vocabulary with a resounding thud. I enter my personal twilight zone and leave the doctor's office through the waiting room, which has morphed into a long, dark tunnel.

Later, at home, I call my best friend, Nelda. "You are kidding, right?" she asked.

"I wish."

She is quiet. She asks me for details and tells me how much better treatment is these days. When she speaks, I hear her voice crack. "We'll beat this thing together," she said.

No, I think. *This is* my *journey.*

An overwhelming need for interaction washes over me. Suddenly I appreciate human touch. Quick hugs from Bob, the kids, and friends take on new meaning. I cry and tell my girlfriends I need them to touch me.

Today women are advised to take responsibility for themselves, their bodies, their medical care. When I research breast cancer, lumpectomies, cancer survival rates, and treatments, I read until my frayed emotions can't take it anymore. I am now a statistic. I log off the computer, weep, and wonder if I will survive.

I try to face my fears and not become paralyzed. When there is no pain, it seems this must be happening to someone else. Yet when I touch my body, I feel the intruder. There it is, small and evil. I read enthusiastically about positive thinking and visualizing good health. I wonder if a difference exists between visualizing and imagining, but I plunge into visualizing healthy pink tissue in my body.

My hand goes often to my breast, where the intruder has entered. Amid plentiful prayers and a measure of denial, I begin to accept the circumstances with the resolve to overcome. When my hand goes to the place, it travels with reverence. I realize, with unabashed concession, I love this ordinary body that has served me so well.

Although I know good health is a blessing and am thankful for it every day, I look back and realize that because I took care of myself by exercising and eating right, I expected to always have good health. My time in front of the mirror is brief because I am always moving on to something else. Fixing up means putting on lipstick and earrings. Pulling my hair into a ponytail so I can ride in the car with the top down is the easiest way to go.

My body still works—and I don't feel much different—so this is all difficult to believe. I try to sort things out. My spirit tries to separate itself from my body. I face mortality and try to define death.

Will I survive this?

I'm not so sure. On June 24, 2005, Dr. Caluda removes the tumor from my left breast, along with the larger tumor from my lymph nodes: fourteen nodes in all, and eleven showed cancer. On June 25 I turn fifty-seven. *How did I survive?*

Although it's a wonderful thing, modern medicine is not perfect. There's no real cure for cancer. My surgeon is good and he knows it; no self-esteem problems there. "Go home and pray," he says as he checks me a week after the surgery. I have been. I do.

A drain tube has been sutured under my arm and must be emptied of blood and fluids twice a day. It's been one of the worst aspects of the ordeal so far. I want it out. My energy and emotions drain out along with the fluid.

I stand in the shower trying to reconcile body and spirit as water flows over and soothes my wound. My body attempts to heal itself and tell its story. I ask Bob to massage my back and arm and, as he does so, I pray his touch will rub the cancer away. He changes my bandage, after which he and Amanda, my daughter, lovingly, gently rub around the area of my surgery. I think of the Book of Luke, the physician, and the way Jesus healed so many with his touch. There must be something there.

My incisions heal quickly. One warm evening here in the Florida Panhandle, Bob and I are swimming in the pool under the stars. I will start chemotherapy in a few weeks.

"I'm scared," I say for the millionth time.

He takes me in his strong arms. "I don't want you to be afraid," he says as the water laps around us. "Remember, your body is only a shell."

"That doesn't help right now. I'm not ready to let it go."

"Don't you want to see your mother and father? Your brother? Don't you want to see them and be with them?"

"Not really, they're dead," I say, feeling I am totally alone. He doesn't get it.

In the bowels of Sacred Heart Hospital, I lie in a twilight sleep. Two male nurses prep me. Dr. G is about to install a Mediport under the thin skin of my chest. One nurse is warm, friendly, and caring.

The other puts his hands on my breasts unnecessarily as he works. I know it's wrong, yet I feel I can do nothing. Tears stream down my face. A couple of hours later, as Bob takes me home, I am in a panic. My chest and neck are taped so tightly I can barely breathe. Something else to survive.

"I had a dream recently," my friend Jeanne says. "I dreamed three different doctors told me I had breast cancer. I was extremely fearful, and I woke up upset. I believe God sent me the dream so I would understand your experience better."

I am quiet. "Thank you," I finally say.

I begin chemotherapy. My hair is falling out in handfuls, so Bob shaves my head Sunday afternoon as my friend Paula sits on the patio with us. When he finishes I look into the large mirror in the bathroom. I push the corners of my mouth up in a smile. It's the only way to survive.

Hair loss is emotionally traumatic, but it's not the worst thing that happens. I manage minor nausea with small meals of comfort food. Fatigue is my middle name. I continue teaching a limited schedule four mornings a week. Teaching gets my mind off myself and my self-pity. By noon I'm on the couch for the rest of day. I lie silently in a kind of trance. Sometimes I put cucumber over my eyes. Sometimes I play soft, whispery music.

I've got all my life to live, I've got all my love to give. And I'll survive, I will survive . . .

I slip into deeper depression and finally accept the prescription for the antidepressant the doctor suggests. During fleeting moments of peace, I remember the spirit never dies. But our bodies are the selves we know. We know what we've seen of death and we don't like it. Death belongs to other people. Somewhere beyond the dreams of spirit and the comfort of touch are healing and peace of mind.

People tell me I am strong. What choice do I have? We do what we must do. Clichés ring of truth, and attitude is everything. We survive when we love, give, and believe.

On January 5, 2006, I receive my last infusion of chemotherapy. I am excited. Three weeks later I notice I can taste my coffee. It's the most delicious taste in the world. Maybe I will survive after all. I still face six weeks of radiation but am confident the worst is over. My son is getting married in March, and I'll be there.

SANDY'S WRATH

by Dr. Cynthia Paulis

In 2012 Halloween came in the middle of the week, so most people celebrated on Saturday. I had attended a costume party at Old Westbury Gardens on Long Island. The evening was warm and mild, with a full moon casting a silver glow on the gardens, which had been filled with five thousand carved pumpkins. There was talk of a hurricane called Sandy that could be "the big one," but we had heard that warning so many times before, and it had always been wrong.

The next day the wind started to howl and the temperature dropped. I went to the beach and watched as the waves churned and threatened in the distance. Kite surfers were taking advantage of the wind, flying with reckless abandon above the waves. Children did cartwheels on the sand and frolicked in front of the sea. Outraged at the mockery, one rogue wave grabbed a small child and dragged him into the ocean, pounding him on the sand, but he was quickly rescued by his dad. Sandy was hungry and angry, but that day none of us could imagine to what degree.

On Monday the wind picked up speed and huge oak trees started to sway and bend to the oncoming storm. People still did not take heed as they walked around laughing. At 4:00 P.M. a power line exploded on my block, setting a tree on fire and knocking out my electricity. The familiar hum of my house went silent. Soon more trees bowed and fell to Sandy's wrath as people scurried into their homes, now with growing concern.

I decided to get extra batteries, just in case, and drove three blocks to Ace Hardware. The line was out the door—not to the hardware store but to the liquor store next door. People were preparing for a hurricane party. None of us yet believed that Sandy would be anything more than a two-day annoyance.

The next day there was massive destruction over three states: New York, New Jersey, and Connecticut. Those who lived by the sea found their homes filled with water in a matter of minutes as the ocean and the bay joined hands and charged onto the land, killing people and sweeping them out to sea. People drowned in their homes. In my neighborhood, houses powered by gas exploded and incinerated in a matter of minutes, while firemen wading through chest-high water could only stand by helplessly and watch them burn.

I had lost contact with the outside world: no land phone, no cell phone, no power, and, worse yet, no heat—only a radio with reports of what was happening outside. The temperature plummeted and my house became extremely cold, but fortunately I still had a house, with no damage and no flooding. The fifty-year-old oak trees surrounding my home held tight to the ground and didn't topple over, unlike so many others that now lay on their sides, roots exposed.

In Massapequa, where I live, I am a mile and a half from the bay, and yet the water came within six blocks of my house. It looked like a war zone outside. Trees had crashed into homes, grabbing onto power lines as they fell. Live wires were popping and crackling, spitting out sparks as they snaked their way across the pavement, littered with debris. Some streets had fish flopping around on the sidewalk, gasping for their last breath. Seaweed coated six-foot fences, marking the height of the storm surge.

Some people were lucky and had power, some had hot water but no heat, some had generators, and some had nothing at all. I had nothing, and I was cold and hungry. I found a deli in town with hot coffee and a Chinese restaurant that was cooking food on a questionable gas wok. How bad could it be? I ordered hot-and-sour soup and shrimp lo mein. Things were not so bad for me until that night, when I realized the Chinese food had given me food poisoning.

Death would have been kinder. I was in so much pain I thought about going to a hospital, but I knew many people had been evacuated because the hospital generators had failed. I couldn't call for an ambulance because the cell-phone towers had been knocked out. I laid on the bathroom floor with the cats coming in and out looking at me as I hugged the porcelain god.

Each day the house got colder, and trying to sleep was difficult as I got better and the food poisoning gradually subsided. Sounds of generators and sirens filled the long, dark nights. I was thrilled to see the sunrise, only to have it vanish by 5:00 P.M. Fuel became a premium, with people waiting five hours in line only to be told there was no gas left. Some stations had gas but couldn't pump it because there was no power. Fights broke out, and the police began patrolling the stations as well as the neighborhoods that were falling victim to a new problem: looters. Driving on a highway was like playing rodeo cowboy, with no traffic lights and everyone speeding.

Just as we were all trying to wrap our heads around the destruction, we were hit with a nor'easter, bringing more cold weather and even snow. Days of darkness and freezing temperatures turned into weeks with no relief in sight. I refused to fail pioneer school 101, so I decided to become more efficient. I lined my bed with flannel sheets and a down comforter, covered it with a plastic tarp to keep in the heat, and grabbed a couple of cats for warmth; they didn't seem to mind.

But soon the cats started to get stressed. They would huddle together at night for warmth and in the morning line up in front of the windows, soaking up the sun. One of my cats, Meiji, who had cancer of the abdomen but still ate, was now missing. I found him hiding under the couch for warmth, but he would no longer eat or drink. This cat was fearless and had received an award in New York City for rescuing my mother, who had Alzheimer's and had wandered off one night, calling my attention to the matter. Meiji had posed for pictures with Caroline Kennedy, Susan Lucci, Cindy Adams, and Morley Safer. He was awarded a Tiffany silver heart with his name engraved to wear proudly. Now he was cowering. Sandy had gotten to him as well.

I took Meiji to the local animal hospital, which was operating by flashlight only because their generator had failed. The news was not good. He was dehydrated and had an infection. We needed to get food into him and keep him warm. It was freezing in the vet's office, so I took him home, wrapped him in blankets, parked the car in the sun, and cranked up the heater full force. I mixed canned salmon with some water and syringed him with the food, which he didn't seem to mind. This became a routine for several days, until he started to eat on his own. I had to stay mindful of the needle on the gas tank, though, since there was no sign of a gas delivery coming to our town.

Three blocks from my home were Ace Hardware and Gino's Pizza, my lifelines to sanity. I ate hot meals at Gino's and filled five Styrofoam cups with hot water to use to towel wash and to drink at night for warmth. I parked myself at Ace Hardware, enjoying the heat and light until they closed. People walked in looking like zombies, all sharing horror stories of Sandy. When supply trucks arrived, all mayhem occurred as batteries and lanterns were grabbed out of boxes and emptied in minutes by desperate customers.

During the day I rode my bike to a local park, where a Red Cross relief center had been set up, and volunteered, distributing food, water, and blankets. On the way to the park I passed home after home with all of its possessions dumped out on the street, reeking of saltwater, sewage, and now mold. A lifetime of memories destined for the dump. It was heartbreaking to see, yet there was one thing that struck me with each person I spoke with. They all seemed to say the same thing: "I was lucky. I was blessed. I survived."

Some had lost everything—house, possessions, and more—yet they had come to the realization that surviving and being with your family and friends was more important. At first many people were frightened and confused by all the destruction. Then, over time, there was a resolve to build again. Cleanups started and trash was hauled away for months as homes were demolished and then rebuilt. Some people never returned. We were a broken island for a long time, and there are still so many parts that will never be the same. Sandy took so much and broke our hearts, but our resolve to live and love again remains strong. As Gloria Gaynor sings in her song, we will survive.

Over time we have gradually come back. The beaches that were gobbled up by the sea have been rebuilt. Dunes flattened by the surge have been raised again. Some seaside restaurants are now open for business, though others have closed forever. Spring rewarded us with prolific blooms of cherry blossoms, dogwoods, and azaleas, lifting our spirits with hope as warm weather returned and the days became longer. Even the trees that had been toppled and lay on their side also came back as willows and oaks sprouted new shoots of green leaves. They, too, like the rest of us, have survived and are determined to start over.

HOME IS WHERE MY FAMILY IS

by Carlie Powers

Congratulations! First Eastern Mortgage is pleased to inform you that your loan request has been approved . . ." the letter began. Like a phoenix rising from the ashes, I had been reborn.

Nearly ten years earlier I had stood in the rain during the foreclosure auction of my marital home, which, by then, the kids had come to know as "Daddy's house," after I had taken them one night and escaped to Grandma's. The thing is, Daddy quit showing up for work during an alcoholic binge and subsequently quit paying the mortgage.

From the driveway, I could see the windows of my office, where I had worked as a marketing-communications consultant, and the windows of the master bedroom, the living room, the dining room, and the family room. I remembered the holidays and "happy" times we had hosted. Then the memories of the dark times descended like a cloud, and I looked away. My eyes rested on the sandbox the boys had played in years before, the mailbox with our name on it. In a few moments, it would all be gone. The faux flowers someone had hung on the front door were the perfect metaphor for my marriage: They looked good, but they were fake, a fraud.

Eighteen months before, when my husband was out of work for the third time in about that many years, our constant togetherness had shone a light on the fact that our marriage was all wrong. He was not the man he'd pretended to be. I wanted to be mistaken. He tried to convince me I was. He tried to convince our marriage counselor to convince me I was. He tried to convince me I was crazy, imagining things, having "false feelings." One of my friends summed it up this way: "The con wore off." And because I had a different point of view than him, the shaming, blaming, and belittling had begun. He could no longer contain his rage, and I feared his mercurial moods. I had a never-ending headache, I was grinding my teeth, and my hair was falling out. The constant angst in the pit of my stomach was suffocating: I couldn't catch my breath.

The night I gave up the charade began like any other, starting with the boys' bath. I then got them dressed and methodically packed them and whatever belongings I could fit in the car and drove away, as I had rehearsed so many times in my mind.

The rain came down harder, and a sudden gust of wind whirled it up under my umbrella onto my face, camouflaging the two tears that had leaked out, one from each eye, as the auctioneer called, "Going once, going twice … sold!"

I shivered. As I walked to my car, got in, and turned around in the driveway for the last time, I remembered a story about a little boy who was watching firemen trying to save his family's burning home. The boy bravely told a neighbor, "That's just a house. Home is where my family is." I headed back home to my family, and home, to Grandma's house.

This chapter of my life was over. In the next my general malaise was transformed into desolation by my utter financial devastation. I hardly had time to grieve the loss of my hopes and dreams because I was so consumed with worry over the loss of most of my possessions and nearly all of my money—including my inheritance, which I had invested in the marital home—followed by my two best clients, as the economy took a turn for the worse. However, since I could barely afford to feed my children, I certainly could not afford to waste time wallowing in self-pity or "if onlys." Failure was not an option. My boys needed someone to count on.

Wishing I didn't have to be the one in charge of "everything," I frequently thought about an earlier time in my life: my own childhood. "I Will Survive" was a song that had been popular when I was a carefree young teen. I would sing it to myself for inspiration when I found it necessary to accept help from our local food pantry, our new church, government programs providing health care or food, or when I shopped at the local supermarket with vouchers—often with people I knew waiting in line behind me.

Because I dared to leave him, my ex-husband tried to destroy me financially. Aside from allowing the foreclosure, he has never in ten years been current on the minimal child support he was ordered to pay. I'd chosen to leave the church my boys and I had attended when Daddy spontaneously began showing up again; it was no longer safe to worship there as his slander against me forced people's loyalties to become divided. Sometimes it felt like the only things I hadn't lost were my hope, my faith, and my reason to go on: my love and devotion to my children. I knew I would do whatever I had to do to take care of them. And I did.

At the time, I couldn't see a way out of the terrible mess I was in, but I knew that worrying was God's job. Actually, what it means is, it is not my job to worry about things—I should be giving my problems over to God. So I quit trying to figure everything out on my own and instead prayed to Him, asking that he show me the path forward. And then a consulting job materialized: a dreadful business-to-business telemarketing job. *Really, God?* I didn't want to do that kind of work at all. I was a writer. This job would mean I'd have to take a career detour. Additionally, I was compelled to shelve my personal writing projects. Yet I had to trust that it was part of the master plan. I'd be able to work from home—not without child care, which in some years consumed a third of my pre-tax income, but without the commute and within close proximity to my children.

I accepted the position and worked at it for a year, smiling and dialing, and as it turned out, it was a stepping-stone to the solid and stable corporate job I have held for the past eight years. Like a phoenix, I had survived the fire and been reborn from the ashes, once again feeling like the happy and confident person I saw in my photo albums from years past.

I wouldn't have picked the route I wound up traveling to get where I am today, but I'm grateful for the rocky road, since that's what it took to get here. *And I'll survive, I will survive, hey, hey!* I thought as I called my Realtor to arrange a showing of one of the houses I liked, so my family and I may begin the next chapter in a home we own.

BONNIE THE WORD FINDER
by T. Marie Nantais

Bonnie grabs the spoon off the table and dances around the dining room. Gloria Gaynor's song "I Will Survive" just began playing on the radio. My sister sings at the top of her lungs and moves the makeshift microphone up near her mouth, swaying it from side to side. She extends her arm outward and points her finger as she reaches the lyrics *Go on now, go, walk out the door* . . . She appears to revel in the power of that line. Her young daughter claps her hands and twirls, as our brother in the other room turns up the volume. His twin sons pick up the beat and laugh along with their older cousin. I watch from the kitchen and can feel a sense of inner strength rise within me, as though with each note belted out from the radio I could accomplish anything.

Then I hear: *Oh, no, not I, I will survive* . . . Bonnie's voice dominates all others. She's a little off-key but doesn't care at all. Everyone joins in, especially for the last *And I'll survive, I will survive, I will survive* . . . And then the room goes silent as the last notes of the song finish. Smiles and hugs all around. Bonnie is so well and happy. Her future awaits her.

Several years have gone by since that electrifying moment, but it all seems like yesterday. Bonnie loved words—both in music and in word-find puzzles. Just over a year ago, I was out shopping and saw a word-find book filled with literary quotes, so I placed it into my basket for Bonnie. I didn't realize how unique a gift this book was until I got home, sat down, and began to browse through its pages.

"This is so neat," I softly said as I flipped from one page to another. "Bonnie will love this."

I decided not to wait for a special occasion but to mail it immediately to my sister. It would be the kind of "just because" gift that Bonnie so much believed in giving. I found tissue paper printed with ruby roses, wrapped the book, and then placed it in an envelope. Some days went by, and then Bonnie phoned.

"Where did you get that word-find? I love it. Thanks. Do you know that each word or word phrase you find is part of a famous quote?"

So, over the next months, Bonnie took her word-find to her cancer-treatment appointments.

One day she called to say, "Today at my appointment a couple of women noticed the word-find, and they loved it. They wanted to know where to get one."

Another conversation followed a few weeks later. Bonnie told me, "I bought another one of those word-finds."

"Which volume?" I asked, because I secretly wanted to get her a different one for her next "just because."

I jotted it down and then she said, "Gotta go. Love you."

"Love you too. Lots." I placed the phone down and tears welled. I hoped she'd be OK. I wanted her to be OK. What if she died? The emotional pain overwhelmed me, and I couldn't stop crying.

As I write this, I have that word-find beside me. It's a little dog-eared, and the top edge of the spine is missing a piece of covering. I open the book and see that Bonnie used a blue pen to cross out each word. Sometimes she'd use one line and, at other times, two or three. It seems she wanted to be complete. I see how precise she was in finishing each word-find word. She never circled the found word but put a straight line through it instead. I always circled the entire word. I keep turning until I am a third of the way into the book. I find her last one. It was nearly finished but incomplete. As I look through the book, I realize Bonnie kept order when doing each word-find. She never did one out of turn. She lived life's events in the same way as a great adventure to behold and share with others. So, I wonder what she went on to do after she closed the book for her last time. Go to her appointment? Take her children to their piano lessons? Finish knitting a sweater?

I can hear her laugh now as I hold the book in one hand and write with the other. Oh, how Bonnie could laugh. She laughed from her deepest insides and tears would sometimes fall from the corners of her eyes. "Oh my goodness!" she'd say with her contagious smile. Bonnie's hands once held this book, and it gave her distraction and inspiration amid her darkest trials. I hold it gently and carefully, for now it's a golden treasure.

She fought her illness triumphantly for three and a half years, but a time came when it was just unbeatable—at least physically. She left a legacy for her youthful children, husband, parents, siblings, nieces and nephews, friends, students, to whom all her love was given.

I think about the many years of childhood I shared with my sister. She played with me in the playpen, read books to me, and stayed at my side an extra night in the hospital when I had my tonsils out. I live each day now without her voice on the other end of the phone or her text messages or special cards in the post. I can't see her or hear her, but I still somehow get through each day. I must. Her loss can't be described in words. There aren't any such words. I take each day—and sometimes each hour—at a time, knowing that she would want me to find peace here not only for myself, but for her children, with whom I was entrusted. I put my feet forward, one in front of the other, each day, sometimes slower than the day before or the day before that, but I keep living and moving with Bonnie always at the forefront of my deepest being.

Shortly after her funeral, I was driving in my car and a song came on the radio that I recognized and that simultaneously conjured feelings of both joy and sadness: It was "I Will Survive."

It's true, really. It happened. I thought about Bonnie and how she outlived the time given to her by the doctors. She kept going.

Since Bonnie's death some people have disappeared from my life, while others have stayed, supportive and loyal. I'm learning—or trying to learn—to live without Bonnie now. The tears still come and the grief is strong, and I yearn to hear her voice. Yet I know what she would say: "Now go on. Help someone today. Don't spend all your time thinking about me. You'll get through this. You'll survive this. I know you will. I love you."

So, in my mind's eye, I take my sister's hand, and I see her walk alongside me. I'm not alone. She turns and looks at me and smiles.

THE ULTIMATE SURVIVAL

by Beckie A. Miller

Throughout my life, Gloria Gaynor's song has reminded me of the power of the human spirit to survive what often feels impossible to survive.

As a child, I survived the sexual abuse of my father, who molested each of his four daughters. I was the oldest and first to endure his ultimate betrayal. More than forty years ago, my sisters and I tried to get help, and yet he was allowed back into our lives by the system to abuse us again and again. Then, in the summer of 2001, all four sisters finally had a chance to truly believe we would survive when our father was finally held accountable and sentenced to prison.

It was not enough to make up for all the years he had gotten away with the abuse. Yet as we banded together in court to obtain justice for our youngest sister—who was disabled and had to endure his abuse for many more years than the others, even into adulthood—we felt validated for the first time in our lives. Now he could not hurt anyone else the way he had hurt us, as long as he was in prison. For me, the freedom of not having to worry anymore that he might be abusing my younger sisters was a wonderful feeling, and I felt an enormous weight lifted from my shoulders.

Still, becoming a survivor from this sort of crime takes a lot of hard work, soul searching, often years of counseling, and, if you're lucky, finding someone who will love you dearly and protect you. I found all of these things in my husband of now forty-two years. Having a son and a daughter and a stable family life has helped me on the path to becoming a survivor more than anything else.

Then, nineteen years into a wonderful marriage in which I had truly found my soul mate and my best friend, a tragedy struck—one that I felt I absolutely could not survive. My eighteen-year-old son, Brian, recently graduated from high school, was robbed and shot to death while walking his girlfriend home in our neighborhood of country mailboxes and stables. The killing took place in the middle of suburban Phoenix, where we had been transferred as a result of my husband's military career and chose to remain.

After Brian's death, many years went by before I could hear the song "I Will Survive" on the radio and believe its message of hope. The pain of losing a child to murder is, on a scale of one to ten, an eleven. There is no worse pain for a parent and no grief like that in the aftermath of your shattered world. Enduring the judicial process—which should have brought justice but instead gave our son's killer only seven years in prison—left our lives and our future irrevocably changed.

Did you think that I would crumble, did you think I would lay down and die?

I did. I imagined just that and often wanted to die—to put an end to the horrific pain that had seared my heart, my body, and my soul with agonizing grief. My husband and daughter were the only reasons I chose to live. Because to end my life, to end the pain, would have meant hurting them more than they had already been hurt. My husband had lost his only son and my daughter her only sibling and best friend. I had to learn all over again to survive. But how? I didn't seem to have the answer.

Despite the fact that songs such as "I Will Survive" are powerful tools in the recovery and healing process, it took more than that for me to heal from this tragedy. I had to find my mission and purpose in living and reclaim my spirit that was, for a time, lost.

Many things would give me that purpose in the coming years, such as the adoption of our youngest daughter as a newborn baby five years after the murder of my son. While one child can never replace another, a new child can give you a reason to open your heart again to the joys of nurturing and loving and the innocence that a child brings.

For years I would hear "I Will Survive" on the radio but never believed I actually might feel like a survivor again. But once my baby daughter was born and placed directly into my arms, I cried tears of absolute joy—something I never thought I would do again. At that moment I knew I would survive.

I've got all my life to live, I've got all my love to give . . .

And that truly is what it is all about, the receiving and giving of love. Love keeps me tied to my son because the cord that was never severed by birth is still nurtured with a love that death can never destroy.

Over the years I have taken on the role of leading the support group Parents of Murdered Children. Helping others to survive similar tragedies is the hardest, most rewarding work I have ever done. It was a journey of great personal challenges and growth, and I found an inner courage I'd never imagined. The group now consists of thousands of survivors who help each other to go on. We take many steps forward and backward, and it is a lifelong journey without full healing. I have now been with the group more than twenty years since Brian was murdered.

I chose to become a survivor, but I did it for my family and to sing my son's silenced song and, I hope, to make a difference in this world for others. That is the ultimate survival lesson.

A LITTLE PIECE OF LEATHER
THAT WAS WELL PUT TOGETHER
by Gloria Gaynor

"OK den, all right den, I'll see you den," Irma, my baby sister, said as she left my house after one of her frequent visits. She moved slowly and tried not to grin, while speaking with a thick, Southern drawl. Irma was imitating an elderly, very Southern aunt of ours, who used to take at least half an hour to say good-bye departing our house.

This sort of scene was common to Irma's demeanor and character. A jokester from the heart, Irma could make you laugh during the most reverent, sad, or traumatic situations. It was one of the things I most admired about her. If you were sad, Irma was sure to be the one who could and would bring you out of it. Irma told jokes with precision, timing, and impeccable delivery.

She was quick-witted and intelligent, like our mother. She was a talented artist, very pretty, slim, loyal, compassionate, loving, thoughtful, fiery, and tough, all at the same time. I called her "a little piece of leather that was well put together." I often found it so strange that I should be the frilly, girly girl, while Irma was the tomboy. Why? Because, throughout our adult lives, she was the thin one who could look good in all the latest fashions yet only wanted to wear jeans and a T-shirt. She also kept her beautiful, thick, healthy hair cut short, so she wouldn't have to deal with it. I was the one who always struggled with my weight and wanted to wear all the latest fashions that seldom came in my size. I also have hair that is a job to manage. But such is life.

Our mother had passed away due to lung cancer when Irma was just nineteen and I was twenty-six. All five of our brothers were married by then and building their own families. I had been performing in the Midwest when I got the news and cried all the way home on my United Airlines flight. I went directly into automatic pilot when I arrived because I was in charge of the funeral arrangements and could not have done it otherwise. The funeral, as I remember it, was jam-packed with my mother's friends, as we don't have a big family. It was very sad, but I remember being unable to cry. I was ashamed because I loved my mother dearly and wanted everyone to know I did, but the tears just would not come. After the funeral I went back to the apartment where my sister and I had lived with my mother. It seemed so cold and empty.

Within the month Irma and I had to move because the apartment we lived in was in a housing project. In these housing developments, a family is not allowed to keep an apartment that has more bedrooms than are absolutely necessary for double occupancy in each bedroom. Our apartment had three bedrooms. So we had to go.

Irma and I found a three-bedroom apartment and lived together until she had her first child and moved into her own apartment with her fiancé. We remained very close and visited each other often through the subsequent years, during which time Irma had three children.

On Irma's frequent visits to see me, she would bring one or more of her three children, unless one or more of them happened to be visiting another relative. We would play games with the kids, and Irma and I would talk about everything. She was a very good conversationalist, with a bit of knowledge about a lot of subjects. We had a lot in common in that we both loved movies, art, amusement parks, and board games. We enjoyed discussing world affairs. We liked to speak about people in general and would often end our conversations discussing man's inhumanity to man. Neither of us could understand which part of "Do unto others as you would have others do unto you" was so difficult for some people to understand. Irma and

I were both quick to come to the rescue and defend anyone we cared about. We were always on the side of the underdog, and Irma was quick to defend anyone she felt had fallen prey to injustice.

Irma came face to face with man's inhumanity to man one fateful Thanksgiving Day in 1995. I had been booked for a singing engagement in South America and spoke to Irma before I left. We had talked about her Thanksgiving Day menu, and I told her that I would not see her there because of my engagement. She understood, as it was one of many holidays I spent on the road during my career. I did my performance in South America, and it went down very well, as, I'm pleased to say, all my shows do there.

When I arrived home, I fully expected I would call my sister Irma to come over and bring me some leftovers. Instead, that Friday after Thanksgiving turned out to be the blackest of Black Fridays I've ever lived through. I arrived home with my husband, Linwood, who was also my manager at the time. My youngest brother, Arthur, met us at the airport, and he was obviously distraught. He told me he had some disturbing news but did not want to get into it until we got home. The one-hour ride was tedious, as he was obviously trying with great difficulty to make light conversation and avoid telling us what was weighing so heavily on his mind. When we arrived at home, Arthur took our coats, as if we were guests in our own home, and led us to the living room, gesturing for us to sit down.

"Now I don't want you to get too upset," he began, "because we didn't tell you this while you were away. But we all [my older brother and he] decided that since there was nothing you could do, nothing anyone could do, we should wait until you got back."

"Wait until we got back to tell us what?" I anxiously asked.

"Well, it's Irma," Arthur said.

"What about Irma?" my husband demanded.

"She's uh, she's uh . . ." Arthur stumbled.

"Uh *what*?!" I yelled.

"She's in a coma."

"She's in a what?!" I shouted, jumping to my feet. *"What do you mean, she's in a coma? Why? What happened?!"*

Now both Arthur and my husband stood and helped me to sit back down while Arthur explained. It seemed Irma was on the way to get some cranberry sauce from the convenience store on the corner near her house when she met a woman who lived in the neighborhood. They started walking and talking together when a guy ran up and began to yell at the woman. Irma kept walking as they argued. When she looked back, the guy hit the woman. Irma yelled at him that he shouldn't be hitting a lady, and the guy became so mad at her that he chased after her. Irma tried to run away, but he caught up with her, punched her to the ground, and stomped her in the head with his big work boot and left her there. Someone called 911. She was already in a coma by the time she reached the hospital.

I cannot tell you how hard it was for me to see my sister in the hospital, in that state. The lively, fun-loving girl I knew was lying there, appearing lifeless. All kinds of machines were hooked up to her frail body to keep her alive. I cried and tried to talk her out of the coma. I brought music and encouraging messages on a tape recorder and played them for her all day. I even asked the nurses to play them all night. I prayed for the Lord to bring Irma out of the coma and back to us. I called my best friend, Fippie, and asked her to pray with me several times.

The last time, Fippie said to me, ever so softly, with all the compassion she could put into her voice, "Gloria, Irma doesn't want to come back."

I did not want to hear that, even though I knew it might be true. As upbeat as my sister was, I knew that the past several years of her life had not been the happiest.

Irma succumbed to her injuries three days later. I don't remember the funeral at all. Again, I went into automatic pilot. I only remember that at the repast following the ceremony, someone played "I Will Survive," and it reminded me of the many times my sister had played the song at my house and told me, "Honey, that is *my* song. It gets me through every sad, mad, or bad situation I ever find myself in. It should by yours too; you're the one who recorded it."

So whenever I'm going through something difficult, I think of my sister and sing our song, along with another song the Lord gave me a few years later, by the same name. The three of them get me through every mad, sad, or bad situation I ever find myself in. No matter what life throws at me, the one thing I'm sure of is that "I Will Survive."

A CAR RIDE TO HEAVEN

by Julie Carson

My husband and I had what I thought was a perfect family. We had three very boyish boys, growing up in a wonderful neighborhood. Billy was my firstborn, and I guess we were anxious for him to have company, because Stephen was born just twenty months later. They were not only close in age, they were nearly inseparable growing up. Although Stephen was a bit younger than Billy, he was the leader and the most mischievous. Stephen was a little rascal who really gave me a run for my money, like the time he cut the phone wires in the middle of my conversation. The two boys kept me busy enough that I waited five years before I had their little brother, James. James was constantly teased by his older brothers, as is often the case with siblings. He always used to say in response, "Wait till I get older, I'll show you."

My husband worked for Con Edison, and I worked my whole life as a bookkeeper. We wanted to make sure all our sons had a good education, so we were determined to keep good jobs. Stephen was the tough type and very protective of his little brother. He was great to have around during an emergency. They all loved sports and would watch TV together in the living room. I remember my sister-in-law saying she could not understand why they seemed to waste so much time watching sports with their dad. I felt it was good, healthy alone time for the boys to bond with their dad, learn good sportsmanship, and other valuable lessons. James's favorite teams were the New York Mets and Jets, the Philadelphia Eagles, Florida State football, and UNC for college basketball.

Those wonderful years of bonding and learning with their dad came to an end when James was just twenty years old. The older boys were already living on their own and James was attending SUNY Oneonta. My husband passed away, and James wanted to make sure I was looked after, so he moved back home to finish college. I was very proud of my youngest son when he received his bachelor's degree in computer science. James had become my world after my husband's death, and I think I became his best friend. He was very concerned for my welfare and very attentive. When I began to date after a few years, I would consult him about my appearance. "Do I look all right, son?" I'd ask. "You look great, Ma," he'd respond. I would do the same when he went out with his girls. Girls loved him. They were constantly calling and sending letters to the house. He had such a strong presence, was mature for his age, and his bright smile was infectious.

Billy and Stephen had married, had good jobs, and several children. I am very close to their wives and consider them my daughters. They are devoted to my sons and great to me. At the age of thirty-two, James had married a wonderful girl named Debbie and was working in Connecticut. He received a call from eSpeed, a part of Cantor Fitzgerald, for a new job. Debbie and I were delighted he might be working closer to home, in Massapequa. They employed him as a computer network administrator on the 103rd floor of the north tower at the World Trade Center in lower Manhattan. Little did we know that his dream job would not turn out to be the blessing we thought it would be.

On that fateful day, September 11, 2001, I received a call from my son Stephen, who worked in Midtown Manhattan. "Ma, turn on the TV," he said frantically. I kept the phone to my ear as I turned on the television, wondering what could possibly be of such interest to me that my son would call me to watch it. Every station had the events live at the World Trade Center. Stephen said, "I don't think James is inside." He did not want me to worry, but to remember that there were several World Trade Center buildings. I could not begin to think the unthinkable. It was surreal. *How could this have happened?*

I questioned, as I incredulously watched the news report. I immediately went into denial. *Lots of people were hurt, but not my son. He wasn't in the building. I didn't know where he was, but he wasn't there. He's only been working there for six weeks,* I reasoned. *He loved it. He's always raving to Debbie about his incredible view. There was no way I would never see my son again.*

Stephen tried to call his brother but could not get through. After a few hours, Stephen called me back. "I think James is in the building," he said.

"Oh my God," I screamed. I went into shock and could not move. It took all the strength I had not to fall apart. I had just seen him two days earlier, at Stephen's house. Soon thereafter Stephen, Bill, Debbie, and some others went into the city to see if they could find James. In the days that followed, I was still in shock and on automatic pilot. I was asked to give my DNA in saliva and hair samples. At that point I knew James did not stand a chance as he worked on the 103rd floor. That whole floor had been wiped out. The phone wires went down so quickly, there was no chance to call him, or for him to call out. The family search party looked everywhere—hospitals, on the streets, and in other buildings. Deep down, we all knew he was gone, but when do you ever think it's forever? Parents aren't supposed to outlive their children. How do you do it? How do you say good-bye when there's no one to say good-bye to? How do you let go?

Debbie and James had only been married two short years. Debbie was Jewish, but she wanted to have a special Mass for James a few weeks later, at St. Christopher's church in Baldwin. She was pregnant with their first child. The outpouring of support from childhood friends, neighbors, teachers, and families was overwhelming. I thought it would just be a few family members. I was still in a state of shock. How would I ever survive this? People came up to me, but I didn't recognize many of them as I hadn't seen them since they were kids. They also had a fund-raiser for Debbie and her unborn baby at a local restaurant. I could not comprehend that James would never see his child, that this child, my grandchild, would not have that special relationship that James's father had with him. No coaching his son's games, no playing his favorite video games with his son. How could I not crumble? How could I not lay down and die?

After the first year, the shock wears off and reality sets in. There were a number of support groups for the families of those lost in the tragedy. When I was ready, I joined a few of them. One was called Compassionate Friends. I also went to my own therapist because I needed it. I felt my sons needed help as well, but they were not interested. I found that unsettling. Through all the help, I kept wishing that this terrible tragedy had happened to me instead. James had a wife, a baby on the way, a beautiful home in Massapequa, and a great job. He had everything to live for.

Little James Matthew was born in March 2002. Debbie made the choice to bring her son up Catholic, something she and my son had discussed previously. I took off from work and helped Debbie with the baby as much as I could. It was during that time together that I heard Gloria Gaynor's recording of "I Will Survive." I knew the song but had not heard it for quite a while. As I began to listen to the once-familiar words, they lifted my spirits. I listened again and again, and each time I felt better. Now it became my mantra. Whenever I begin to feel a bit down, I play the song, and it encourages and inspires me.

I am able to enjoy seeing the many mannerisms my little grandson James seems to have gotten from his father. He has his daddy's eyes as well. Often when I would give him a bottle I would look at his daddy's photo on the mantel and smile at the similarities. I have given Debbie all that I had left of James, except the things I'm hoping to share with James Matthew when he is ready. One of those things is a message I saved from my answering machine of James's voice. When Debbie and James Matthew visited the WTC he asked his mom if they could get a second car to visit his dad in heaven.

Some families who suffered loss on 9/11 are still receiving body parts and have had to reopen their loved ones' caskets to bury them. I received nothing, and I believe James would have wanted it that way. I have a plaque in our church to honor James and a bench in Long

Beach, and I donate to different groups in his memory. It was simply his time, and I've had to let him go, although I will never let go of the wonderful memories he made so indelibly for his family—most of all me. Life is full of sorrow, but I thank God every day that I have my family and James Matthew to keep reminding me that I will survive.

FACE VALUE

by Carol Harper

The first time I heard Gloria Gaynor's song "I Will Survive," I was lying in my bed, too depressed to move. I had just gotten home from another surgery to rebuild facial bones that were crushed to powder in a car crash. I had survived the hundred-mile-an-hour impact, and hearing her upbeat tune inspired me.

Before my life-changing car crash, I was a vivacious, beautiful young lady with a successful career. As a public relations assistant at a prestigious hotel in Washington, DC, I wined and dined high-profile celebrities as well as congressmen and senators. My looks were a very important part of my job, and I attended all the black-tie events at the hotel, including the Inaugural Ball.

A few years later, I relocated to Atlanta and met the man of my dreams. He was handsome, had a great job, and we fell in love. We got married and were very happy for the first year. Then tragedy struck. I was on my way to work on July 7, 1979, when a drunk driver hit me head-on. My face was ripped from my skull, leaving me unrecognizable.

The hospital called my husband and, when he arrived, the doctor told him that my facial bones had been crushed and I was in critical condition due to a traumatic brain injury. My nose and jaw were broken and I'd lost the sight in my left eye. When my husband walked into the intensive-care unit, he saw a woman whose head was twice its normal size. I was black and blue and so swollen that he didn't recognize me. He told the doctor, "That is not my wife," but when the doctor showed him my wedding rings, he broke down and cried.

During the month I was in the hospital, the mirrors were covered because the doctors thought I would be devastated if I saw myself. When I got home and looked in the mirror for the first time, I saw a face that was not my own. The first words to come out of my mouth were "I'm ruined." I was hysterical and wished I had died in that car crash. When my facial bones were shattered, my self-esteem was shattered too; I had always based my self-worth on my beautiful face.

I was totally dependent on my husband for three months. I couldn't walk by myself, fix my own soup, take a bath, or wash my hair. I had to suck soup using a spoon because my mouth had been wired shut. It took over an hour to finish a bowl of soup. My once-shapely figure was now skin and bones.

My days were spent in bed, crying my eyes out and trying to adjust to my new life. On the radio I heard Gloria's song, "I Will Survive." It gave me strength, and I knew I was going to get through this tough time in my life. Although the song is about surviving a broken relationship, I could identify with the words "I will survive." I kept singing them over and over again. Hearing those words empowered me.

The doctors performed five additional surgeries to rebuild my face, but I never looked the same. They took a piece of hip bone to reconstruct my nose and pieces of Teflon replaced the cheekbones that had been blown away. After every surgery, ironically, I kept hearing Gloria's song, "I Will Survive." It was like God was playing it personally for me. I found it so encouraging, and I would always sing along with Gloria. It felt like God saved my life for a reason, and I was determined to find out why.

My neurosurgeon told me that because of my brain injury and short-term memory loss, I would not be able to work again. Then my marriage ended when my husband had an affair. I loved my husband, and it hurt terribly to be betrayed. I cried until my eyes were red and swollen. But if I survived the car crash, I could survive my divorce. I would cry and sing the words to Gloria's song. The louder I played the song, the more empowered I became.

Although my marriage ended, I had a baby girl who kept me going. My daughter and I lived on the income from my part-time telemarketing job, and I received some child support. My daughter and I went through some tough times financially, but God always provided. Many times I felt like I was hanging on by a thread, but God held me up. That car crash made me a deeper and more spiritual person.

When my daughter graduated from high school in 2001, I wanted to do something with my life. Mothers Against Drunk Driving had a Victim Impact Panel in which victims tell their stories. I was nervous, petrified of public speaking, but I wanted to speak at MADD. Determined to overcome my fear, I joined Toastmasters, a public-speaking organization. After two years in Toastmasters, I joined the Victim Impact Panel for MADD and have been speaking there for eight years. After each time I speak, several convicted drunk drivers tell me they will never drink and drive again.

If I had not gone through this near-death experience, I would not be an author or speaker today. I found my purpose by looking inward, instead of concentrating on my outward appearance. I now judge others by who they are inside and not by their looks. My own self-esteem is healthier now that it comes from within.

My current goal is to speak to women about healthy self-esteem. I want to empower women to love and respect themselves and not depend on men to give them their self-worth. I intend to play "I Will Survive" before I am introduced. I think that will empower the audience as it empowered me.

KICKING UP OUR HEELS

by Linda O'Connell

Rose, Millie, Judy, and I headed into our forties with equal amounts of uncertainty, fear, and wild abandon as we simultaneously terminated our long-term marriages. We were at a pivotal point in our lives, afraid and unsure about what we really wanted. One thing we knew for certain, though, was that what we had wanted when we were eighteen—to get married right away—wasn't what we wanted anymore. We were on a quest to discover what we were missing, and Gloria Gaynor accompanied us on our collective journey.

The four of us fondly referred to "the Summer of Our Lives" as a period of enlightenment and self-discovery, and wondered if we could actually survive on our own. Those few months left us intoxicated with newfound freedom and resulted in unparalleled personal growth. We encouraged one another, listened, laughed, linked arms, and marched in lockstep to the beat of our own drums. We danced the summer nights and our worries away on the patio of an open-air bar and grill as Gloria repeatedly belted out our mantra, "I Will Survive." Ms. Gaynor was instrumental in getting us through that turbulent Summer of Our Lives.

By this time all of our kids had left home or were nearly grown and doing their own thing, so we had few constraints. Each night we headed to Chips—a little neighborhood bar and grill, which was nothing like the New York and LA clubs we'd heard about. Chips was a comfortable establishment, like Cheers, the bar on the television sitcom. Everybody did know our names. As regulars, we had our own bodyguard—Millie's brother worked there.

Chips was our ticket to fun. The outdoor patio featured mediocre food, cheap drinks, pitchers of beer or soda, and a wild and crazy disc jockey who spun 45 rpm records—those black vinyl discs. Being outside was better than being in a stuffy, smoke-filled club. The night air cooled our perspiring bodies and smoke wafted away on the breeze, instead of stinking up our clothes and hair. The stars and moon illuminated our nights, offering far better ambience than a dimly lit barroom.

By day, my girlfriends and I assumed our everyday roles in our workplaces. We wore sensible footwear: flats, low heels, and sneakers. But when the sun went down we were like kids itching for some fun. We called one another to coordinate our outfits and sexy high-heeled shoes, the ones we kept in our closets for special occasions. Sometimes we wore open-toe strappy heels or peekaboo toes. We wore low heels, pumps, or four-inch spikes in every pastel and bold color. We wore them with jeans, strapless dresses, and even shorts as we headed out for a few hours of healthy fun, beneficial exercise, and social activity. Our shoes defined us. When we slid our pedicured feet into our dance shoes, we strode with confidence, crossed our ankles with flair, and flaunted our calves. We shaved our legs every day—the same legs we'd allowed to stubble when we had husbands and harried lives.

Every evening at eight o'clock we arrived together and piled our purses and beverages on one of the round, plastic picnic tables. For the next three to four hours we gabbed and gazed at youthful hard bodies. We flounced and flirted under the sky. Dancers crowded onto the concrete dance floor underneath a covered pavilion. The disco ball flashed overhead as the DJ joked and played everything from old-time rock 'n' roll to Top 40 hits. Oh, that eighties music! Patrons, who ranged in age from their early twenties to early fifties, rubbed elbows and pelvises, bumping and grinding to the beat.

We sang at the top of our lungs, freestyle danced together, and boldly declared that this was going to be our year. Each night we came and left as a quartet. Occasionally we assumed aliases when we had

GLORIA GAYNOR and SUE CARSWELL

to fend off a freak, but mostly the atmosphere was fun and friendly. We rocked to Rod Stewart as he crooned his tunes in that hoarse, sexy voice, but it was Gloria Gaynor who infused us with the strength to make it through one more day. Her lyrics spoke to us.

At first, I was afraid, I was petrified . . .

Every time we heard this, we'd look at one another knowingly, nod imperceptibly, shove our chairs back, and beat a path to the dance floor. Every time the tempo climbed, it swept our minds and bodies into a frenzy. We belted out every word. When Gloria sang "I Will Survive!" it was as if she were championing us, imploring us to move forward into the unknown and leave the misery behind. We asked the DJ to replay her No. 1 hit several times a night so we could get our fix.

We literally danced our heels off. When we wore our plastic high-heel caps down to the metal, we continued to dance. It looked like flint striking on rock, and the sparks flew . . . primitive pyrotechnics to enhance Gloria Gaynor's vocals.

By the time autumn shed its last leaves, the four of us had let go of many of our insecurities. Dancing just wasn't the same, though, when the music moved indoors. We drifted, not apart but into different lifestyles. Even before winter wrapped itself around our town, we'd given up high heels and nights out. Instead of burning the candle at both ends, we snuggled on our sofas in front of the fire. We settled in and down to a new way of living, but with a newfound confidence. Before long we'd all developed positive, healthy relationships, and every one of us eventually remarried.

And then, exactly a decade after the Summer of Our Lives, I lost two of my dear friends to cancer and another to a sudden heart attack. I couldn't imagine how I would survive without them. They had been there for me during the toughest times of my life.

The lyrics to Gloria Gaynor's song "I Will Survive" again helped me get through a crisis, this time through some of the worst periods of mourning. I envisioned my friends and me as younger women with big hair, kicking up our heels night after night, laughing, dancing, and coming into our own.

With the death of my girlfriends came the realization that life is too short for us not to pursue the things that make us happiest. With no formal training, I began my freelance writing career. I simply wrote from my heart about how Rose's friendship, in particular, affected me not only in life but even after her death. She sent me a flower in winter per our pact. My essays have been published in seventeen books and more than a hundred national and regional publications.

I never dreamed I would lose my friends prematurely (yes, fifties and early sixties seems young to me), but then again, I never dreamed I'd have such success as a writer. I left a two-day-a-week job at a small private school and accepted a teaching position at a public school. Life moved forward, yet I felt so alone.

I met and married the man of my dreams. We have a blended family of four adult children and nine grandchildren, all of whom give me lots of laugh lines. In my heart I believe that every day truly is a gift, and no matter what comes my way, I know for a fact, as Ms. Gaynor crooned many a night to me and my girlfriends . . . *I will survive.*

IN SPITE OF IT ALL

by Nadia Ali

I stood petrified by the side of the road. Cars sped past. Pedestrians hurried by, unconcerned about the tears streaming down my cheeks. "How can I go on? How can I survive?" I repeatedly asked myself. He is not my husband or even a boyfriend—he is my *son*, my own flesh and blood! I recalled his hurtful insults and crushing words: "Move out! I am selling this house!"

But it was my house, our house, our family home. Surely memories were worth more than the market price? Tears fell uncontrollably down my face. Alone, scared, and broken, I wondered how I was ever going to learn to get along.

I clutched the plastic grocery bags filled with my things and made my way to social services. Stripped of my dignity, embarrassed, and dismayed, I felt the reality hit me hard and had to say the words aloud: "I am homeless. My son sold my own home out from underneath me." My voice trembled, and I was unable to look into the eyes of the person behind the desk.

"We'll find something for you, don't you worry," came the caring response.

It didn't take long before I was shown a place to stay.

"This is your room," said the attendant. It was a simple room that had the distinctive smell of disinfectant. The furniture was old and the curtains looked like a resting place for spiders.

"You can put your things in the drawers, and I'll come back to see you later," instructed the attendant. It was a far cry from my beautiful, four-bedroom family home.

As I lay down, the actions of my son haunted me. Sam was the youngest of my four children. He became an architect and had successfully worked his way into a top position in an international company overseas. I recalled the immense pride I felt seeing him in his cap and gown when he graduated from his university. I had watched him go from strength to strength toward the top of the career ladder. Little did I know that when he asked me to sign a document that was supposed to give me a lower mortgage rate, I was really signing over the family home to him.

I couldn't contain my sadness; my tears fell relentlessly. I couldn't believe this was happening after everything I'd gone through—losing my mother as a child, getting divorced, and saying good-bye to my three other children, who had gotten married and gone abroad to live. I had struggled to secure a mortgage on the family home by myself and worked hard to maintain the payments. Sam was well aware of all of this. He was there to see the struggle it took for me to acquire my own home. He was the one for whom I'd sacrificed the most, putting him through university and helping him to become the success he was today.

Now, in a strange room, I could hear the words of Gloria Gaynor's "I Will Survive" in my head. The lines mimicked real life—*my life*! I vowed to live the rest of it . . . and I grew strong, and I learned how to get along . . . I'd begin in my new surroundings, with my new neighbors, in my new life. With each passing day it was hard not to think about the home I'd lost with just one simple signature. It became such a blur—days meshed into nights and nights back into days. I never told anyone why I was there—not the other tenants, not friends, not family and, most of all, not my other children. I couldn't bring myself to talk about it. I just couldn't.

One morning, a few weeks later, familiar keys slipped into my fingers from my handbag; they were the keys to my old house. Maybe, just maybe, I could go back and collect more of my things. In a bold move, I made my way toward the phone and began to dial my old home phone number. I hung up before it connected, and then hesitantly dialed again. This time I heard the ringing on and on and on. No one was at home.

With a sudden burst of energy I left, making my way to *my house.* I stood poised at the door and gently put the key into the lock. It opened and I walked in. I felt like a criminal entering my own house. Furniture was missing, the walls were bare, and there were no more trinkets or appliances on the kitchen countertops. He had already begun to empty out the house to sell it.

"Oh, it's you," came the sound of a male voice behind me. Sam stood with folded arms. "What are you doing here?" he coldly asked.

"It's my house!" I declared.

"Have you come to take things away?" he smirked. "It's already been sold, so why don't you just turn around and walk out the door?"

I looked into his eyes in disbelief. There was no emotion in him. No connection. Was this really my own son speaking to me in such a heartless manner?

"Go on," Sam instructed. "You're not welcome here anymore!"

I sternly looked at him and said, "Are you trying to hurt me with your words? Do you think I'll crumble? Do you think I'll simply lie down and die?" My voice got louder as I gathered my courage and took a step toward him. "I have spent so many nights just thinking how you did me wrong and I used to cry, but now, Sam, now, I hold my head up high." I pushed past him. "I will survive, Sam!" I made my way out, leaving the front door open behind me.

The pain of being ousted from my own home faded over the years as I learned to appreciate my new life. I became settled, comforted, and, as I had promised myself, I grew strong, having learned how to get along.

From time to time I welcome my other children and my granddaughters into my new home. As for Sam, he has never made the effort to contact me again. I am thankful that I still have all of my life to live and I have all my love to give . . . and I survived!

BROKEN ANGEL

by Cheri Jalbert

For Ayla Bell Reynolds. Missing from Waterville, Maine, December 2011. We are still praying for you to come home.

She died in my arms. The light faded from a spirit so illuminated with sunshine that it had almost caused physical pain to watch as it disappeared. Angel, the young sister of my heart—a girl who had dared me to become a better person—slipped silently away in that moment. It would haunt me forever that she spent her last breath in a dirty alley reeking of urine and garbage.

Piercing screams echoed around the alley, sending the remaining street people scurrying. It took a few minutes to realize the sounds came from deep within my soul. The agony of her loss nearly ripped me in two. We'd been kindred spirits. How would I survive without her?

Sirens shrieked in the distance. Someone tugged on my sleeve and motioned toward the oncoming parade of EMS vehicles. They were too late. In my world they had always been just a little too late. I laid Angel gently on the ground and covered her with my jacket, tucking the edges around her tiny frame. It could easily have been me a few years ago.

I stood and made my escape as the first cruiser turned into the alley. They would have questions. I had no answers. Locked enclosures didn't agree with me. I'd been bounced around in enough of them to have lost any kind of faith in the system. Upon my graduation from high school just a few months earlier, I'd finally earned my long-awaited freedom.

I watched from a distance as they lifted her onto the gurney. Tears scalded my skin as I tried to focus on the car I'd caught throwing Angel's lifeless body onto the cold tar. She'd been pale, lifeless, and covered in vomit.

I went back to the alley dazed and blaming myself for not keeping a better eye on Angel when a car made a hasty exit. I had to jump back or be hit. The man driving was in his midtwenties, had dark hair, and wore a panicked expression. The car was dark, maybe blue or black, but it had a dealer plate on the back. It quickly squealed away.

Angel had been a fourteen-year-old runaway, trying to survive years of being passed around by the adult males in her family. I bumped into her one night while walking to the store. She'd been living in the alley behind my apartment. I found her fighting off a guy twice her size. From that moment on, I tried to watch out for her.

The memory nearly made me smile—until the sudden approach of oncoming headlights had me ducking into the shadows. My heart nearly stopped as a familiar vehicle crept past the alley. The same man sat behind the wheel. His head moved like a bobblehead doll, trying to see everywhere at once. Rage seared my throat as I ran to my car. Trapped at a red light, he tapped his fingers restlessly against the steering wheel.

He took off as soon as the light changed, and I followed him as closely as I could. After a twenty-minute drive, I pulled into a large car dealership and slid into a row of parked cars. The modern-styled building was deserted. He entered a glittering dome of glass and cement and locked the door behind him.

Once inside, he walked over to an older, heavyset man who paced near the display window. Sneaking from my car, I ran closer to where they stood. The tension between them radiated as I watched them argue, throwing their hands in the air, shouting at each other.

The heavyset man handed the younger guy something. He let it drop to the floor as he held up his hands and shook his head. The heavyset man pointed his finger in his face, shook it, motioned to the packet on the floor, then turned and marched away down a long corridor, leaving the younger man standing there. A few minutes later, he bent to retrieve the packet and slid it into his pocket. He shook his head and turned toward the door. By the time he reached it, I was already in my car, waiting for my chance to escape. As soon as his car turned out of the lot, I left in the opposite direction. During the drive home, a plan began to form in my mind. There had to be a way I could find out how Angel and these men were connected, or why the man in the dealership had dumped her body as she lay dying.

I dressed carefully the next day. Something bad was going on at that car dealership. It had cost Angel her life. The same heavyset man I'd seen the night before answered my job inquiry. He introduced himself as the manager and, as luck would have it, they were hiring. I took that as an omen to continue.

I was to be a "runner," someone who delivered cars from point A to point B. Sometimes the cars were traded, sometimes they were delivered to customers at work. Occasionally the dealership just liked having someone drive around with the name of the company in the windows to bring in free advertising. Being near Angel's murderers fed the wound that constantly festered inside me. Watching them smile and carry on with their lives, as if her death didn't matter, brought me to my knees. These men had gotten Angel and many others hooked on heroin, and when Angel OD'd, they'd dumped her body back in the alley where she lived. They knew no one would be looking for her. She was just another street kid in their minds.

One day I sat hunched in a bathroom stall, wiping tears from my face, as the second verse of "I Will Survive" echoed over the speakers throughout the dealership. Because Angel and I had both left dangerous family situations to survive, this had become our theme song. We'd sing it to one another to get through the rough patches . . . *I'll survive, I will survive.*

A warm feeling snaked up and down my spine as the familiar lyrics began to comfort me. It was as if Angel had whispered in my ear, "Girl, get off your butt and fight. Fight for both of us."

The next day, Tom, the manager, called me into his office. My knees shook so badly I was sure I would give myself away. Instead of getting caught, however, I got a promotion. There were certain customers who received special "gifts" at prearranged locations. It seemed that I would be their new delivery girl.

My instructions were to drive to a specific location and leave the car for twenty minutes. Under no circumstances was I to have any contact with anyone at the drop point. If I did as instructed, well, there would be better opportunities for me and lots more money.

A month later an invitation to a private party was tucked inside the envelope with my paycheck. When I walked in, people were everywhere, doing things I'd never imagined. Two young girls hung on the arms of Tom and an older man. The girls were glassy-eyed and stumbling, and I could see they were completely out of it. Angel's last moments suddenly became clearer.

I tossed back a shot of Jack, stalling, while Tom slid a mirror with fine white powder in my direction. Acid swirled in my gut. My participation was expected. I was in too deep to turn back now. The police had closed Angel's file, just another overdose of an underage Jane Doe.

Weeks later I found myself staring into a raging river at four in the morning. Blood gushed from one nostril and stained my shirt. I'd grown to hate the parties nearly as much as my reflection in the mirror. I whispered the words to our song and prayed to survive the next few hours.

The next day I went to the police and tried to report what I knew. They basically laughed me out of the precinct. Why couldn't I make them understand? Unless that dealership was shut down, it wouldn't be long before more underage girls would meet with the same fate as Angel. I couldn't stand by and watch it happen again.

A few nights later a stranger cornered me. There was something different about him. Something dangerous. He had dark eyes that could pierce your soul. When he spoke, it sent chills down my spine. He had an aura about him that demanded respect.

He showed me his badge and explained that he was an undercover officer for the police department I had been to earlier. A friend had called him after I'd left and filled him in on what I'd said about the car dealership. He had been investigating a string of young girls who seemed to be connected to the dealership. He asked me for my help. He needed a way to get inside to the main people involved and couldn't get any closer unless I vouched for him. He promised me if I helped him, he would help me find justice for Angel, and he did. I knew Angel had had something to do with those men.

Within weeks the car dealership was closed down by the police. I got myself clean and moved to a different state. It didn't end the way I'd wanted. There wasn't enough evidence to send anyone to jail for Angel's death, but the vehicle that caused it was gone forever. It would have to be enough.

Thirty years later, Angel's memory is still fresh in my mind every time I see an AMBER Alert or hear Gloria Gaynor's song. I'm one of the lucky ones, one of the few who survived the monsters in the darkness. It haunts me that others are lost forever. My thoughts and prayers are with them, hoping that somewhere out there they find the strength to hold on, just a little longer.

LIFE WASN'T THROUGH WITH ME YET

by Wanda M. Argersinger

She was our first. She could have been our last. Yet there was something inside that told me to keep trying, as things weren't over yet.

Stephanie was born in 1973. The doctors immediately knew that something was wrong. It would take two weeks, one more hospital, and a trip to Houston, Texas, to know what that something was. *Cancer.* She lasted three short months. It ended not only a young life but also the dreams of a young couple.

We never got to bring Stephanie home from the hospital. We never got to dress her in anything other than hospital wear. We never got to bathe her. We never got to do a lot of things we thought we would. We cried. We prayed. And, on occasion, we believed. But it was all in vain. When Stephanie died that October, we lost so much.

Not only had we lost our first child, we were buried in medical debt. Lost in the moment of trying to save our child, we'd had no idea how the bills were mounting up or how they would ever be paid. We were naïve.

But things weren't over yet. For some reason the dreams didn't die with Stephanie, and the bills didn't kill us.

In 1974 Daniel was born, the continuation of a dream that was almost lost. He was beautiful. He was loved. We were happy.

For three years we would be a family, allowing ourselves to believe that life was good and we had not only found a little piece of joy, but that we deserved it.

In 1977 our second son, Adam, arrived. But as soon as he was born he was whisked away to the pediatric intensive care. He was not the color of a healthy baby. He was not pink or crying for his mother. No, Adam was a very dark shade of blue, almost to the point of being black. His little heart was failing to pump the oxygen-rich blood his little body needed.

I was in the hospital for three days. When we left, Adam did not leave with my husband and me. Once again I was going home without my child. I was entrusting someone else with his life. I thought I had forgotten the feelings that engulfed me when I left the hospital without Stephanie. I was wrong. When I went home without Adam, I was swallowed by grief, fear, depression, and the knowledge of what dark possibilities the future might bring.

I knew too much and not enough. I asked questions. I tried to understand. And I cried.

The doctors told us that Adam had a problem with his heart. When he was awake everything operated as it should, but when Adam was asleep—which was most of the time—his little heart beat irregularly. I heard words like "heart problem," "lack of oxygen," and "rare condition." No one knew for sure what the future held. What I heard was all too familiar to me.

Adam was finally released from the hospital, and we took him home. We loved him. We tried to live a normal life.

If you looked at us, we seemed much like every other young family. There was a daddy, a mommy, and two beautiful children. What you couldn't see was the anguish, the hurt, the fear, the doubts, and all of the questions.

If I hadn't asked it enough with Stephanie, I asked it far too much with Adam. What did I do wrong? What could I have done to prevent this? Why can't I take his place?

Of course there were no answers. The doctors didn't have any. Our minister didn't have any. Our parents didn't have any. So, day by day, we simply survived.

I held Adam as much as possible—partly out of fear, partly because I could feel his heartbeat. I could feel when things were normal, and I could feel when the beats were irregular. I was the first to know that the problem was gone. I felt it first with my hand and second with my heart.

I knew even before the doctor read the EKG and told me Adam had outgrown the condition. I heard the words. I knew them to be true, and yet I still lived in doubt.

In 1979 Daniel, our perfect child with no problems, developed an eye condition. We were sent to a specialist who didn't know our history. He said, "It can be anything from a birth defect to a brain tumor."

All I heard was brain tumor.

We had to wait two weeks before an MRI could be performed to determine the problem. We spent two weeks in a dark place. I could barely move from the couch each day. I was overcome by the possibility that fear, doubt, and depression had become my companions.

The results came in and, thankfully, Daniel was pronounced healthy. The reason for the premature diagnosis was a birth defect. Daniel was a large baby, and the pressure he experienced during birth had caused a pseudopapilledema that looked like a tumor, putting pressure on the back of his eye.

Was it ever going to end? Would the roller coaster ever stop? Could I get off and not give up life? Could I be a mother to my sons and be happy?

Little did I know that the strength I needed to survive—as well as the answers I was seeking—were in a song that had been released a few months before Daniel's first diagnosis. A beautiful song titled "I Will Survive" had been playing on the radio. For a while it was just that—a beautiful song about the breakup of a man and woman. But when I was sent to that dark place of worry, fear, and depression, I heard the words that cut through the gloom.

Like Gloria Gaynor, I survived. My sons survived. Our family survived.

It was a struggle. It took a lot of hard work. It wasn't easy, but I made it. We made it. From the darkness and depression and fear, we survived.

Today I have two beautiful sons, three beautiful grandsons, one gorgeous granddaughter, and a precious, happy family.

THE PAINTING

by Nancy Vogl

It has been reframed—much like the reframing of my life, putting the pieces of my soul back one fragile fragment at a time. The delicate watercolor strokes of burnt orange, mustard, cranberry, cornflower blue, and olive form a palette of poppies, forget-me-nots, and greenery on textured paper, matted with complementary hues.

The picture hangs inconspicuously on my living-room wall, grouped with two other watercolors. Its significance is known only to me, unless I tell the story, purposefully pointing out to the casual observer the unusual marks embedded in the background and in three of the flowers.

There are eleven tiny tears randomly carved in the painting, caused by yet another long fit of turbulence, when it was flung across the room and the glass shattered into hundreds of pieces.

The shards of glass, like the shards of anger and hatred that once fractured my spirit, I allow to remain embedded in the painting because I want to always remember. While I've set much of that particular event aside as merely a bad memory, coupled with a heavy dose of forgiveness, I don't ever want to completely forget. I want . . . I *need* to be reminded of where I've been, what I've overcome, and where I want to go.

It happened on a snowy evening between Christmas and New Year's, many years ago. A few days before, he wouldn't—or perhaps couldn't—give me any money to buy presents for our daughters until just two days before Christmas. I know he relished the fact that I had to wait. The stress of running around to make another Christmas as magical as possible for my sweet babies in such a short amount of time was just too much; I collapsed with a flulike illness on December 26, unable to care for my daughters or our small town house.

Still sick a few days later, I laid for hours in the easy chair in our tiny living room, drifting in and out, in a state of minimal awareness. He came home sometime that evening, bringing the children back from my mother's. A simple sentence, nothing out of the ordinary or unkind, induced the episode. He had put the baby on the floor next to me to take off her snowsuit and change her diaper before bed. Through bleary eyes I saw him putting the diaper on backward, with the plastic against her skin, and casually alerted him. Just like countless times before, the simplest of things would set him off. He rose like a fierce dragon rearing its ugly head, charging at me vocally with every mental and emotional bullet he could fire.

I have little memory of what happened next. I do remember the children crying, hearing loud crashing noises, the room spinning, then total darkness. I must have passed out from fear and horror. I don't know how long I was out, but while in that state I heard an inner voice telling me I was slipping away, that I was dying internally. The voice continued: *You're sick enough now. Do you want this to manifest into even more serious physical ailments? Do you want your children to grow up seeing you so incredibly unhappy all the time? If you don't find the courage to make changes in your life NOW—for your health and for the sake of the children—then when? When, when, when?*

I awoke several hours later, sometime late into the night. Everything was silent and peaceful. Oddly, I felt worlds better than I had in days. I was on the verge of a change.

Making my way up the stairs to check on my girls, I found them all fast asleep; the baby was in her crib in the little corner room, while the two older ones were each in their beds in the room they shared. He, however, was face down on the floor between the two older girls' beds, still in the same clothes from the day before, snoring loudly. Had he been drunk? And how did the children manage to get to bed safe and sound during that terrible tornado of madness?

Feeling energized, I decided to stay up for the rest of the night. I cleaned the messy house, did the dishes, cleaned the laundry, re-arranged the Christmas clutter, picked up the myriad of things that had been thrown around by him hours earlier, and thought about what to do next.

While cleaning up the living room, I stooped to pick up the shattered glass and broken frame that had housed my little painting and discovered the damage—to the painting, as well as to the very core of my being.

It was the final blow, and it brought me to my knees. I'd bought the painting at an art fair, drawn by its simple beauty. It served as a symbol of the kind of life I yearned for—uncluttered, full of grace, sur-rounded by love that was tender and real. I wanted no more sudden fits of jealousy, no more rash moments of rage, no more towering angles of power where he would push me against a wall and force my shoulders back until they felt stretched out of their sockets, all the while screaming down at me at the top of his lungs. I desperately craved happiness. I wanted to know what it was like to feel pure joy and, more than anything, I yearned for peace—soft, silent, tranquil moments of peace.

Holding my precious watercolor against my chest, I suddenly opened up to the reality that I could no longer live with the constant fear, the tension I felt each time I heard him pull into the driveway, always trying to anticipate which way the pendulum of emotions would be swinging that day. My heart and soul simply knew: Now was the time.

At 6:30 that morning I stood over him while he was still on the floor next to our oldest daughter's bed. It was the first time I could ever remember feeling a sense of power over him. I nudged him lightly with my right foot, causing him to roll over and look up at me through bloodshot eyes. I announced resolutely, "I am getting a divorce, and there is nothing you can do or say to ever, *ever* make me change my mind." As I walked out of the room, feeling light and free, as if a huge block of cement had been lifted off my shoulders, the lyrics from the song "I Will Survive" swirled in my head.

I'm not that chained up little person still in love with you . . .

Taking charge once and for all of what I truly desired, of who I wanted to be, who I hoped I *could* be, I remained firm in my resolve. He finally left after three long, drawn-out days of promising he would change, that things would be different. Yes, things *would be* different, but this time it was me making the change and taking control.

Eventually the little painting of lovely flowers found a new layer of protective glass and it has traveled to several different walls as I continue moving forward, discovering who I am and what I want in the process. It has been more than twenty-five years since I picked up the pieces of my shattered life, and I've slowly been piecing them back together.

Today the painting hangs wherever I'm supposed to be. Tomorrow it will hang where I'm supposed to go. And the reframed shards of my life will continue to heal a little more each day, because simplicity, grace, happiness, joy, and peace . . . sweet, sweet peace are now mine.

TESS'S RECIPE FOR A LONG LIFE

by Kay Cavanaugh

The small-framed woman stood at the screen door. "Git yerself in here afore you fry your brains, lady," she yelled to me. "How come ya ain't got no sun bonnet on? Don't ya know that sun will drop ya like a sack of manure?" That was my introduction to Ms. Tess.

Tess's doctor had wanted me to stop by to assess the elderly woman's health, and to see how well she was managing life alone up in Millers Holler. Tess, a ninety-seven-year-old woman, lived in a small, one-level, white-framed house.

As I took it upon myself to get in out of the harmful rays of the sun before my brains were fried like a skillet full of chicken livers, the first thing I noticed was the smell of fresh-baked bread. My taste buds immediately perked up, awaiting an invitation.

Many hardwood trees and more flowers than I had ever seen outside a funeral parlor surrounded the small home. Red and yellow rosebushes, lavender hydrangeas, marigolds, deep purple lilacs, gladiola, and multicolored wildflowers blanketed the small, neatly trimmed yard. Inside the house I noted she had the basics for comfortable living. A light-beige sofa, a dark-brown recliner, two pine rocking chairs, a maple-colored coffee table, and two end tables filled her living room. Her kitchen, which my nose was insisting I visit, held a small oak table with two captain's chairs, a small white stove, and a refrigerator. And there on the clean white counter sat three loaves of recently baked bread on cooling racks. I had to order my brain to continue on with my assessment rather than linger on thoughts of stuffing that bread, loaf by loaf, into my mouth. My stomach growled at my decision.

"I knew ya was comin' to see me, so I baked us some bread. Ya do eat bread, don't ya?" Looking me over, she added, "Ya look kind of scrawny, like ya don't git much bread."

"Oh, yes, Ms. Tess, I do indeed like and eat bread. I could knock those three loaves off before you could blink your eyes," I replied. She threw her head back and laughed heartily.

Tess is a small woman, with clear, sky-blue eyes and a healthy head of cloud-white hair. The many wrinkles on her face looked like road maps to somewhere, and I was interested in where. I sensed that Tess was alert and quick-witted, a woman very much in charge of her life and home. She had a steely, determined look in her eyes. "Set yerself down there and fire away them questions that's popping around in yer head. Ya came to see if this ol' lady is still got all her marbles and ken still take care of herself, didn't ya?" she asked.

"Yes, Ms. Tess. And I do want to know how you are feeling and see if you need any help with anything around the house or yourself. Like who takes care of your yard and all those pretty flowers for you?"

Laughing, she answered, "Chil', I wish I could tell ya I got me a boyfriend who comes by and tends it fer me, but I do it myself. Keeps my heart ticking like a water pump. Ain't nothin' like smellin' fresh-cut grass and diggin' in my flower gardens. I'll cut ya some flowers afore ya leave."

"Tell me, Tess, how do you keep yourself so healthy and fit? Your blood pressure is normal, your weight is good, your vision and hearing clear. What's your secret?"

"Well, chil', I'll tell ya. Ya gotta keep 'em bones movin'. I clean my house myself, mow the grass, even growed me a garden. If yer out there workin' in God's earth, you don't got time to worry 'bout no aching bones. I got that mule out there that heps me haul things. Emmalou, my goat, fer milk. Bake my own bread. Et canned vegetables from my garden all winter. Pray in my Bible every day, and of course my boyfriend Sammy [ninety-five] and me drink a little white lightnin' every Tuesday night. 'Course music is good for the soul too. We likes music, but can't say as I likes that new racket they plays on the radio today, 'ceptin' that 'I Will Survive' song. It perks you up purty good if you takes a notion to start lettin' thangs gitcha down."

"What do you do when you get a cold, flu, or some other health problem?"

"Well, I jest don't git too much sickness. Too mean, I reckon. Done scart the germs off," she said laughingly. "I did have a wart on my knee 'bout two years ago. Took me a green walnut shell and rubbed that on it, and then buried the shell and the durn thing fell off and never came back. I pick elderberries and make me some tea out of that to ward off a cold in the winter. Chew me some of that mint ya see growing in the yard if my stomach gits upset. I also et me a mess of ramps in the spring . . . them cleans my blood. Sammy brangs me sassafras and ginseng roots, and I boil that up and drink that too. But can't say I ever been bad sick. Just walk the earth, et good, pray to God, and set out there on the swang at sunset and look at them beautiful mountains. I don't worry none 'bout no dying, either. I'm ninety-seven. Figure, like that gal says, 'as long as I know how to love I know I'll stay alive,' and God'll take me when he's good and ready. Long as I ken keep myself up, I'm happy. Ya ken live to be ninety-seven too, chil'. Just do what ya ken to keep lovin' an' movin'. Now, ya want some of that bread with homemade butter and strawberry jam?"

"I'll race you to the kitchen," I responded.

Watching this elderly yet spry woman up and about, seeing her ability to take care of herself and her home, I knew she was in good hands—her own. She was a survivor.

After filling up on bread and fresh lemonade, she walked me to my car, promising to get in touch with me if she needed anything. As I drove off I heard her strong voice yell, "Git yerself a ninety-five-year-ol' boyfriend and some ginseng, gal, and ya'll do all right. Jest fine."

I smiled as I drove away from this delightful woman. I had seen many patients younger than Ms. Tess who couldn't do what she did. She was a pleasure to meet and chat with. The ginseng was something

I *would* consider. As for the ninety-five-year-old boyfriend? *I'll have to give that a lot of thought*, I said to myself as I watched Ms. Tess in my rearview mirror, waving until I was out of sight. There's one thing she said that I can and will heed though . . . as long as I know how to love, I know I'll stay alive. With that I'm sure, like Tess, "I Will Survive."

BLESSED, NOT LUCKY

by Michelle Deerfield

People who know me are aware that I may have been called a lot of things in my life, but silent was never one of them. Yet on November 13, 2006, my husband of thirteen years tried to silence me with a .40 caliber bullet to my chest. Fortunately, I lived to tell my story.

I'm not really sure I ever considered what a domestic-violence victim looked like, but I never thought it was the person staring back at me from the mirror. Wasn't it the uneducated person from the wrong side of the tracks with no self-esteem? Didn't that person get beaten on a regular basis and continually take the spouse back, only to be beaten again and again and again? Well, if that's what you think, think again. I am a domestic-violence victim, and I don't fit that profile. Let me say it again: *I am a domestic-violence victim.*

That was hard for me to say for a long time. After my husband, Scott, shot me and was charged with assault and battery with intent to kill—as well as criminal domestic violence high and aggravated—I struggled with that label . . . *criminal domestic-violence victim*?

I tried to explain it to anyone who would listen. I'd say, "But it wasn't a 'normal domestic violence' situation. He wasn't abusive throughout our marriage." And although I still think that's important to note, it doesn't change the fact that I am a domestic-violence victim. It only takes one time, and for me that one time could have been fatal.

For most of our marriage, Scott moved from job to job, unable to keep steady employment for more than a year at a time. Back then I reasoned that it was because he was in the coaching profession, which is often unreliable. I know now that I just wasn't being honest with myself, that Scott's work ethic was to blame. For the last two years of our marriage, he began dealing with some mental-health issues. I had sought help for him through many local agencies, but he would not follow through on prescribed medications and tried to turn the focus of counseling to me.

On March 15, 2005, he held me at gunpoint in a car and threatened to kill me if I did not reveal information about who was sabotaging his professional career. I had no such information and feared that he would kill me. After a horrifying hour-long ride around Murrells Inlet, South Carolina, I was able to escape the car at a convenience store and call the police. Scott eventually turned himself in and was charged with domestic violence.

I left the home we lived in and began seeking a divorce. I told his mother, "He may kill me, but I will not live like this any longer." I had no idea how grave the situation really was.

We began negotiating a property settlement in an effort to divorce amicably. I hired an attorney and had separation papers drawn up. After several times presenting papers to Scott for signature only to have him make changes and request new papers, I had what I felt was the final agreement. Scott agreed to sign them and have them notarized so they could be filed by my attorney. During the weekend of November 10–12, 2006, Scott called and sent me numerous text messages, asking me to meet him in person to pick up the signed papers.

After attempts to meet him at the public library and a local sports bar failed, Scott requested that I come to the home where I had once lived (I was now staying elsewhere) on the morning of November 13, 2006. He said he had a meeting and wanted me to trim his hair. I did not think this was an unusual request, as I had done this on many other occasions—both before and during the separation—and hoped to keep the peace with him.

After arriving at the home at about 7:00 A.M., I trimmed Scott's hair in the master bathroom and asked him to retrieve the separation papers. He went to the garage to get them out of the car but came back without them. He said he didn't know where he'd put them but went back into the garage again for a second look. This time he brought some papers in but said he had made some changes and began shuffling through them. I told him that I had to go to work and that he would have to get them to me later. He told me to wait and stepped into the master bedroom and returned with a gun.

Without saying a word, he fired one shot, hitting the right side of my chest. I fell to the floor and immediately struggled to get out of the house. I was able to get to a neighbor's house and rang the doorbell frantically. No one answered, so I staggered to the front yard in hopes of a passing car seeing me. As I fell to the ground, Scott came out and dragged me back to the front door of the neighbor's house. "Oh, no," he said, "you're not staying out here where someone will find you." I pressed the panic button on my car keys; Scott grabbed them from me and left me lying on the sidewalk. I again tried to ring the neighbor's doorbell but again did not get an answer. I heard Scott coming and lay back down in an attempt to appear dead or unconscious. Scott lifted me up to see where he had shot me, patted around my chest area, then dropped me back to the ground and left me lying there. I believe he thought I was dead. When I was sure he was gone, I got up and staggered toward the golf course behind our house.

I heard a lawn mower coming and followed the sound. I can remember the way the trees and sky looked. Everything was blurry and seemed to be swaying. My ears were ringing, and I was afraid I was going to pass out before I could get help. I hurried to the lawn mower and told the man "I've been shot. My husband shot me. Call 911."

The golf-course worker immediately dialed 911 while I tried to hide behind the lawn mower, curling up in the fetal position on the cart path. Then Scott appeared and demanded that the man hang up the phone. The man did and backed away from the mower. When he was a safe distance away, the man spoke with the 911 operator.

Scott stood over me for what seemed like forever. He rambled on about how he felt I had wronged him. He told me, "I'm going to kill you, and then I'm going to kill myself. We're both going to die today." As I lay on the golf course, believing that this was my last day, I began to recite the Lord's Prayer. I could not imagine how relatives like my niece and nephew would ever understand. I prayed to God to please let me live so that they would not have to try to understand why the person I was married to for thirteen years—the man they had called Uncle Scott—had shot and killed me.

However, I was prepared to die if it was my time. I reviewed my life and felt that I was right with God. I had not left anything undone. I had not hurt someone that I knew of without trying to repair it. I had always made sure that I told my friends and family that I loved them. I was prepared but didn't want to leave this burden on my family and friends. I felt myself drifting and wondering, *am I dying or simply passing out from the pain?* I kept thinking *I can't leave them like this. I can't die like this.* Then the words from the song that had helped me through my difficult separation came to me: *I will survive . . . I will survive . . .*

At some point a police officer had arrived in the backyard and Scott had moved toward him. Soon another officer was at my side. He asked me for the names and phone numbers of family members or someone local he could call. I managed to give numbers for my mom and a friend and begged him to assure them that I would be OK. The paramedics soon arrived, and a helicopter landed on the golf course and flew me to the Medical University of South Carolina (MUSC) Trauma Center. In the helicopter, I kept repeating to myself, "Did you think I'd crumble, did you think I'd lay down and die?"

As I later discovered, the ER nurses were shocked that I was the victim. They didn't think I fit the "profile." One nurse remarked, "Someone shot *her*? She looks like a soccer mom."

When my family arrived from Newberry, South Carolina, they were told that the bullet had entered the right side of my chest, broken two ribs, collapsed my lung, and lodged in my liver. MUSC took excellent care of me, and eight days later I was discharged. The bullet had begun to work its way out of my liver and protruded from my back. It was removed two weeks later. I still do not have full lung capacity and have had follow-up surgery to repair holes in my diaphragm, but have been healing very well over the years. I always have pain in the area where I was shot, but I choose to think of it as a reminder of my survival. I learned a lot of lessons from this ordeal.

A positive attitude can make all the difference. Some people ask how I remain so upbeat after this. I tell them I had two options: I could curl up in a corner in the fetal position and die, or I could move on and live my life. I chose the latter.

Many people have told me that I'm lucky to be alive. I believe I am blessed, not lucky. The most precious blessing that has come from this traumatic event is the man I am married to now. He is kind, caring, considerate, and loving. He has been in law enforcement for twenty-eight years and also brought an amazing stepson into my world. I am truly blessed.

Scott was given a twenty-year sentence but will come up for parole in 2015, nine years after he was arrested for trying to kill me. He'll be released by 2020.

The life I have now is worth every minute of pain I had to go through in 2006, because now I'm saving all my loving for someone who's loving me. I have survived.

A MIRACLE BROUGHT ME BACK TO MYSELF

by Lucinda Stitt

On a hot July Wednesday in 2004, the sound of the gavel jerked me from emotional numbness. Pinal County Superior Court Judge Kelly Marie Robertson had just sentenced my firstborn, Brian, to thirty years in the Arizona Department of Corrections—prison. I had been expecting ten years, as prosecuting attorney Sylvia Lafferty had offered in the plea agreement—not half my son's life! However, Robertson decided to give Brian—who was thirty-four years old at the time—ten years for each of the four counts of attempted child molestation, the first two counts to be served concurrently and the last two consecutively.

Certainly Brian had committed horrible crimes against children and must suffer the consequences of his actions—but thirty years? Three decades? It seemed excessive to me, too much for a mother to take in. This was his first time in any kind of trouble, except for getting caught in junior high school sharing a cigarette behind the bleachers.

Brian is my special child. He has a learning disability and has always needed help in school and in life. He doesn't catch on like others his age, although this is by no means an excuse for what he did. Brian loved children, and they loved him. In fact, because of his learning disability, Brian was very childlike himself. The mothers of the three girls involved in the case had brought them and their siblings to Brian's apartment many times for him to care for while they went out. Sometimes the children even stayed overnight. At some point Brian made a wrong decision—a *very* wrong decision.

After the gavel sounded on that hot July day, I turned to my youngest son, Daniel, to verify what I'd heard. Yes, he told me. The next thing I heard broke my heart. Brian, in an orange jumpsuit and wrist and ankle shackles, turned to the prison guard and asked, "Can I go home with my mom, now?" He didn't understand. I cried bitterly as he left with the guard. I sat for a while, then slowly rose and left the courtroom, wiping tears from my face with my sleeve. I now knew full well why Gloria Gaynor sang, "It took all the strength I had not to fall apart." I did feel sorry for myself.

The next three hours were blank as I drove the 185 miles back to Cottonwood, Arizona. I'd driven the route so many times over the previous two years, since Apache Junction police officers had arrested Brian, that I almost knew it by heart. Every time he appeared in court, I was there.

Once home, my motions felt rote as I skipped dinner and dressed for bed. I tossed and turned, dozing briefly only to be shocked awake, thinking of my son. The next morning I went to work and sat at my desk in the *Cottonwood Journal Extra* office, staring at the computer screen, fingers poised on the keyboard and notes next to me. Nothing. I couldn't write. I couldn't think to write. By lunch, Jane, my co-worker, said, "Why don't you go home and rest?" I agreed.

Instead of going home, though, I turned in the opposite direction and drove to my church. Father Bud Pelletier was available. For the next ninety minutes we talked—or rather, I talked. I spilled the whole story. It was the first time I'd related it to anyone. We prayed, and he told me to place my pain on the altar at Mass on Sunday and give it to God—not as a sacrifice but to have him take it away. "He has big shoulders," Father Bud said.

Driving back to Cottonwood, tears in my eyes and a crushing ache in my heart, I looked up at Mingus Mountain looming in front of me. The sun was bright and on its descent. The cottonwood trees sparkled as the breeze rustled their leaves. I thought more about the song "I Will Survive" and the fact that when singing live, Gloria Gaynor sings, "only the *Lord* could give me strength not to fall apart." I took a deep breath and sighed. "Lord, I can't wait five more days. I can't bear this. Please, please take this pain from me. I can't live with it any longer. Take it now."

At home I couldn't sit still. I moved from one chair to another, only to jump back up a few seconds later. I needed to move. I needed to go somewhere, but where? It was late, and in a small town like Cottonwood most places were closed—except two: Denny's and Walmart. I opted for Walmart. On the way in, I grabbed a shopping cart, although I wasn't sure why. I had no plans to shop.

Mechanically going through the aisles of clothing, household goods, electronics, cosmetics, and candy, I found myself in the garden area, near the houseplants. On the end of an aisle were several plants of a type I'd never before seen. The trunk was braided and the top had clusters of long, dark-green leaves. I asked an associate nearby what it was. She said it was a money tree. I looked at the plant, admiring its unusual shape, and thought I should buy one and get rich. I smiled at my own joke.

Like a two-by-four across my head, I realized I was feeling like my old self. The horrible pain of debilitating numbness and deep black grief was gone. I looked for it, but it was nowhere within me. Immediately, I sent up thanks to God. The associate I had talked with turned and looked at me. God had taken my pain away, and only a few hours after I asked. That pain has never returned in the intervening nine years.

I slept soundly and drove to work the next morning with newfound hope and energy. I wrote three news articles with ease.

Like most difficult times people face throughout life, I knew I would survive this—through faith and love. As long as I know how to love, I'll stay alive, and not only survive but thrive. I have a lot of life left to live and a lot of love still to give, especially to Brian.

The day of Brian's sentencing was the last day I cried, except when a dear friend died suddenly in 2008, and on the day in August 2009 when my sister called to tell me our mother, Corinne, had died after a short battle with cancer. It's not that I've become hard-hearted. It's that I realized through the experience with Brian that some issues are out of our control. Anger and tears are often a waste of energy. That energy can be put to more productive use.

I also realized that prayers do get answered and miracles do happen—every day. We only have to ask.

STRENGTH FROM WITHIN

by Valerie Benko

I t's like slipping into a slow hell.

The nurse sets down the package containing the needle and IV tube. Grabbing my arm, she turns it over and begins inspecting the veins. Frowning, she moves to my hand. There aren't very many good spots to choose from.

She tightens a tourniquet around my arm and my pulse quickens. A vein appears with a little coaxing. She tears open an alcohol-wipe packet and scours the spot. My free hand leaves a moist area on the arm of the chair as I move it to my lap. To my relief she releases the tourniquet, then prepares to insert the needle. I try to disappear into the chair, but it doesn't work. I opt to hold my breath. The IV is in with little pain.

I sink into the chair upon exhaling, and she hooks the IV bag of steroids to the tube and sets the pump.

"You're all set," she says. And then she's gone.

It takes only minutes for the fluid to travel from the vein in my arm to the roof of my mouth, filling it with an acrid taste. I forget about this part and reach for my purse to see if I have gum on hand. Everything I eat or drink will taste metallic for the next week.

A news anchor's voice drifts from the TV mounted on the wall. My eyelids grow heavy. It feels so good to shut my eyes. Did they put a sedative in my IV bag? I don't remember being this sleepy before.

An hour later the drip is done and the machine beeps, signaling the nurse to return. I am freed from my temporary prison. She tapes gauze to my arm where the IV was. Removing the tape later hurts worse than the IV, and the residue will remain for weeks as it resists being scrubbed off.

At home I fire up my laptop and try to focus on work, but I'm still sleepy. I e-mail my boss and tell him I can't work today and drag myself to the couch. As sleep quickly wraps me in its tight embrace, I have a fleeting fear that I will never wake up again.

Tomorrow I'll return for another treatment. It will be a little worse than today's. The day after that will be even more so. By the time this treatment is done, the muscles in my legs will hurt too severely to walk, and my tortured soul will be ready to surrender to the demons in scrubs. Just at that moment they'll release me with a smile, and I will go home to spend weeks healing, only to return in several months, or a year, to go through the misery all over again.

Like Gloria Gaynor's inspirational song "I Will Survive," I always do.

When I was born, my parents named me Valerie, which means "strength," and I was going to need it for the life I would live. My twin sister wasn't so fortunate, dying before I ever got a chance to know her.

For the first nine months of my life I lived in darkness, unable— or unwilling—to see the world around me. Sight came later. One of my earliest memories is of my father's strong hands cracking open walnuts. He was so mighty that sometimes he would squeeze a nut in one hand until its shell cracked wide open. Holding his palm outstretched, I would pick the walnut pieces from the cracked shell. He'd smile at me, alcohol wafting from his breath. Later I would hide as those same strong hands beat my mother.

But I survived.

During the summer of my junior year of college, on the Fourth of July, I was involved in a car crash. As the nation celebrated its independence, I began fighting for my life as an ambulance rushed me to the hospital.

Strapped to a backboard, searing pain tore through my skull. Tears soaked my cheeks. ER nurses fidgeted as they waited to hear if

I was going to be airlifted to a more advanced hospital. The call came to stabilize me there. The neurologist would see me in the morning.

I protested as a nurse cut off my clothes, horrified that I would no longer have the precious shirt I went all the way to DC to buy. Still strapped to the backboard, however, I couldn't resist. She walked away with my shredded clothes and, when she reappeared, I glimpsed a needle in her hand.

"No!"

It was too late. The needle plunged into my thigh, sending fire down my leg. Fog descended, and somewhere through the haze I heard the words, "brain swelling, concussion." Then came the words that would forever change my life: "broken neck."

Later that evening my mother would return home from a trip, to a blinking red light on her answering machine. She'd hit play and listen to a message that would bring her to her knees.

At first I couldn't feed myself, bathe myself, or move unassisted. It would take seven months for me to recover. In that time a deep-rooted fear of being in another accident twined around my soul.

Somehow I survived and even learned to walk again. The neurologist called it a "miracle."

Nine years later I sat in a different neurologist's office, staring at a crack in the floor, while he gave me the answer to why my legs kept going numb and why, for the second time in my life, I had temporarily lost my vision.

"You have multiple sclerosis."

The crack grew blurry as I digested his words. I didn't like the taste.

"How do I treat it?"

"With weekly injections. A nurse will come show you."

More nurses. More needles. A permanent IV pole in my house.

I dreaded the day that nurse came. Nerves wracked my body as she unloaded her little house of horrors onto my kitchen table—needles, more needles, gauze, bandages, alcohol wipes, and a NERF ball to practice on.

Fleeing to the bathroom, I hid while my stomach churned. I didn't want to do this! I'm strong, but not strong enough to stick a needle in my leg.

Coaxed back to the kitchen, we practiced on the NERF ball. She told me the ball was like my leg and the needle would glide through like butter. I didn't believe the validity of her words.

Almost an hour later I nearly froze off my leg with an ice pack before giving myself my first injection. The bite of the ice on virgin skin was worth every second because I did not feel the needle.

It *was* like butter, and I was strong enough, if only for that day.

On the eve of my hundredth injection, I celebrated with a cake. I truly never thought I would make it that far.

I survived. I always will.

STRIVE, SURVIVE

by Lara Marikit S. Tierra

When I was little, to have fish fried in cooking oil, instead of cooked directly in coal, made me feel rich. Every bite was special because we couldn't afford to buy cooking oil. My father was a fisherman who owned a manually operated small boat made of wood, and my mother was a housewife. The only source of our livelihood was fishing. Fish was our viand almost every day. Sometimes my father would barter his catch for a kilo of rice.

When I was in grade school, I used to wrap my cooked rice with fish on top, using a cut banana leaf formed like an envelope for my lunch. All along I thought it was normal. But when I saw my classmates using plastic food containers, I sensed that something was different about my family, and I told myself maybe it was because we were poor. We lived in a nipa hut without electricity. Food was scarce, and we could only watch television programs through the window of our neighbor's house. Sometimes the mood of our neighbor shifted, and she would close her windows, even when we were seriously entranced.

I had a realization based on observation: only those who had graduated from school went on to live a more comfortable life. I wanted to live a better life. I didn't want to grow old, poor, and be a fisherman forever. My brother and I would swim in the deep sea of Sigaboy, Davao Oriental, to find a catch using my father's boat and to sell it to our neighbors, or to anyone else who was interested in buying.

One day my father said, "Marikit, you must stop going to school now!"

"Why should I stop? Even without an allowance, I go to school diligently," I said. Education was free in grade school for six years, and we only paid a little amount for school contributions. I firmly said "No" to my father. I became heavyhearted to hear that my mother agreed with my father. She said that school had nothing to do with our lives, and I would only end up getting married. I didn't believe them. I continued going to school until I finished sixth grade.

I tried to convince my father to let me go to high school, but he was firm in his decision. I told my parents that if they didn't allow me to study, I would leave and find a way.

I left our home at the age of thirteen. I went to the city with empty pockets and five pieces of worn-out clothing in heavy plastic bags. I knocked on every door and asked anyone who answered if he or she needed a helper who was also a student. Most of them refused, and I often told myself that maybe my parents were right. But I couldn't just go home.

One day I took a rest in one of the stores I'd passed along the way. I bought cold water, contained in a plastic bag, for only one peso. While taking a sip, I heard the song "I Will Survive" playing on the radio. I will never forget the lyrics that became instilled in my mind and embedded in my heart. The only lesson that I had to remember was to love what I do and I will surely make it. The song communicated to me that I should pursue my dreams.

So, I continued my search for a home that would accept me as a helper.

Finally I found one. A landlady in a boardinghouse kindly told me that she could provide me a place to stay, but that I'd have to work for it. She could give me free food, but a school allowance was not included. I agreed to her conditions and everything went well. I even asked her boarders if they would allow me to do their laundry for them in exchange for money for school. The bachelor teacher grabbed my offer. I was glad that the force of nature conspired with my plans. I could now afford to pay for my personal needs and school requirements.

To study and work at such a young age was not easy. Tremendous trials came my way, but I had to survive. As Gloria Gaynor sang, "*And I spent, oh, so many nights just feeling sorry for myself, I used to cry but now I hold my head up high.*" With these thoughts, I dealt with the problems I encountered at school with bleeding courage. We were deprived of many things while there—good food, technology, and communication with our families—and endured endless physical exercises that left us exhausted.

At school there was a married couple—both teachers—whom I thought were affluent because of the luxurious clothes and accessories they wore and the car they drove. I aspired to work for them, and luckily they accepted me. And so I moved to their home. How ironic it was, because all the things that I had imagined were exactly the opposite. They were not rich. In fact, they were gamblers. I decided to return to my previous employer, the landlady who had first accepted me. She welcomed me without hesitation, and I remained with her until I finished high school.

One of my teachers told me about a scholarship sponsored by a politician in our area. My teacher asked me to fill out some documents, and she processed the scholarship. Fortunately it was granted and, as a result, I was able to go to college. I finished my four-year degree in elementary education and soon after graduation passed the teacher's board.

I landed my first job as a substitute teacher in a public school. Positions available for full-time teachers were limited, and I was not that fortunate. So I became a saleslady at the mall, where I met the man destined to become my husband. We were blessed with two kids, and we have a simple, happy life.

Still, my desire for greener pastures remained. I applied to the local law-enforcement agency and passed all the written exams, as well as the agility test. I endured the rigorous training at the academy for six long months away from my family. My physical and emotional being were tested, but I successfully finished the training. Happily, I was assigned to the city where my family resides. My career in law enforcement has only just begun, but I know I have the instinct to survive, and that my imagination will always lead me to the next step.

JUST BY TALKING
by Lisa Leshaw

It was my first real promotion at my first real job, and I was beaming. From a sixteen-year-old cashier with her well-rehearsed customer greeting, "Welcome, and how may I serve you today?" to the seventeen-year-old dipper of chicken (flour to batter to flour to fryer), I'd successfully made my way through French fries and onion rings.

I took on the role of dining-room captain only days after my eighteenth birthday. It sounds impressive, but in reality there were only a few tables for me to maintain. Yet it was here in this very small seating area that I mastered the art of conversation, honing my social skills, becoming more personable and much more observant.

It may have all started with a basic "Hi, folks, may I take that tray for you?" But through this simple task day after day, I began to learn that life is not so simple for many people.

I watched the mother who helped her learning-disabled son color the pictures on our paper menu every afternoon. The little red-haired boy favored the blue Crayolas, so I made sure all the little crayon boxes lost their supply of greens and yellows.

I remember an adoring wife who hand-fed her husband but never took the time to feed herself. I'd wrap up her meal and add a little surprise to brighten her day, perhaps a chocolate-chip cookie or maybe an apple pastry.

Then there was the old man in tattered green overalls who always took the corner booth closest to the soda fountain and never said a word to anyone except me, when I'd offer to refill his drink. He'd thank me in his gravelly voice and try to give me a dollar. I always returned it with a smile and a silly joke I had looked up the night before in my brother's joke book for just this occasion. He never laughed out loud, but I could see in his eyes that he was smiling. I also knew that he was happy because the next day there'd always be another dollar and another joke.

Months passed in this veritable training ground.

One day a little girl's spilled fruit punch brought an unexpected opportunity. Her mother furiously mopped up the table and chastised the child for her carelessness, telling her there would be nothing more to drink. I walked past and picked up the plastic cup from the floor. I also took a moment to compliment the mother on her beautiful blouse. She touched her chest and calmed down immediately. I had managed to distract and pull her from her tailspin. I brought the little girl another drink and refilled the mother's coffee. They stayed to spin the tiny tops that accompanied the kid's meal.

I didn't realize it at the time, but this one simple gesture had taught me something invaluable. You can change a situation just by talking to someone.

The way I had been handling my duties in the dining room had not gone unnoticed, because one day the general manager summoned me to his inner sanctum and offered me my first real promotion. I was to be the new assistant manager at the front end. It was a big moment for a nineteen-year-old.

I was issued my new name tag, my new employee staff shirt, slacks, and a contract stipulating my salary increase of $1.85 an hour. I ran to the restroom to put on my new uniform and emerged moments later feeling a whole lot more important and infinitely more proud.

If I could have strutted I would have, but there was no time, because my boss then asked me to join him on a routine supply run to our nearby sister store. I hopped in the car feeling more like a VIP on her way to a red-carpet event than an assistant manager en route to pick up toilet paper and paper towels.

A few minutes later, we veered off the main highway in an un-familiar direction. I figured we were on a back route until the car stopped alongside a heavily wooded area. My boss leaned past me and locked the car door. He put his arm around my shoulder and pulled me toward him. I think he said something about finding me attractive. I probably should have screamed.

Instead I thought back to that earlier day when a few words of mine calmed a mother so she in turn could calm her child. I told my boss he was so handsome that every girl I knew dreamed of one day marrying him. I convinced him that my parents were away and that right after I finished my shift he could come home with me.

He nodded and headed back to the highway, smiling all the way. I had talked my way out of it, at least for the moment.

When we arrived back at the restaurant, I left through the rear employee entrance. I had been an assistant manager for a little over forty-five minutes. In that period of time I had experienced the elation that comes with accomplishment and the heartache that comes with betrayal.

I didn't cry. I didn't call anyone. I just started walking, never to return to the restaurant again.

A car pulled alongside me, or so I thought. I started to shake until I realized the driver was only trying to make a turn into the 7-Eleven parking lot I was now walking past.

Her car radio was blasting and Gloria Gaynor was telling the world that she would survive. If I didn't know better, I would have thought God had tuned the dial to that exact radio station at that exact moment so I could hear the message meant for me.

I bought Gloria Gaynor's record the next day, after receiving my final paycheck. I listened to her song for hours on end and finally came to believe in the words we were singing together.

It had been my dining-room captain skills that eventually gave me the courage to work with people in trouble. I became a therapist. I taught those in need that they could do something I myself had learned to do.

Survive.

REBIRTH

by Marlena Thompson

When I first heard "I Will Survive" in 1978, I immediately made the title of that song my personal mantra, like millions of other women at the time. I sang it while driving, showering, and, most importantly, whenever the stirrings of a leftover heartache threatened to lay me low. At the time, I applied the spirit of that glorious anthem to female empowerment strictly to my relationships, vowing to survive the painful experiences I'd had with men who had cheated, lied, or otherwise left me feeling humiliated and alone.

I succeeded in surviving the losers and abusers and, not long after Gloria Gaynor's courage-rallying song was released, I married for the second time. My husband was truly special, possessing that old-fashioned but ever-admirable quality known as character.

But almost a quarter of a century later I would learn the song held even deeper meaning when a series of crises hit that made betrayal and rejection by faithless lovers seem, if not insignificant, then at least frivolous by comparison.

Though several events occurred in quick succession, it was the first of these that nearly brought our entire country to its knees, as well as impacted me directly. I refer to 9/11, when we were attacked in New York, Washington, and Pennsylvania.

My husband, Steve, who'd worked in the Pentagon for fifteen years, was in the building during the attack. He survived, but later told me that if the plane had veered ten feet to the left, he would have been among the immediate casualties. Still, I believe he was an uncounted victim of 9/11. He lost many colleagues—some of whom were also friends—and attended funeral after funeral over several months. Although Steve was careful not to let work associates see the emotional toll the attack had taken on him—he was raised in a time and place that discouraged public displays of feelings—he was unable to hide his anguish at home. Not being a psychiatrist, I couldn't give a clinical diagnosis for what I observed, but I witnessed what I believed were symptoms of PTSD—post-traumatic stress disorder: stormy outbursts of unprovoked anger, nightmares, and bouts of unexpected tearfulness. Steve had never cried during all the years of our marriage, not even when our baby daughter was diagnosed with autism.

He also suffered survivor's guilt. After returning from the funeral of a colleague and friend—in whose office he would have been at the time of the attack, had a morning meeting not been postponed—he said, "By rights, I should have been buried today too."

I begged Steve to seek out the counseling available to those who, like him, had survived the attack. But he refused, believing counseling to be an admission of "weakness." Yet I knew he needed professional support, so I continued pleading with him to give it a try. He finally agreed. Late in the summer of 2002, as the first anniversary of the attack approached, the media featured stories about survivors reporting various symptoms of PTSD, some of which were physical. Perhaps reading about how others were similarly affected helped convince Steve that counseling was not shameful and could help. He confessed he'd been suffering from chest pains and thought these might be an "anniversary reaction." But he'd also had a history of heart issues, so he promised to get counseling—right after having his heart checked out.

Although Steve got a clean bill of health regarding his heart, the doctors discovered a node in his lung. The node turned out to be stage 4 lung cancer. I was in the room when the doctor uttered those terrible words, and I remember experiencing an intense pain just below my own heart. It was as if I'd received a staggering punch and had the air knocked out of me. I doubled over and struggled for breath.

I recovered and resolved to beat the dire prognosis. He—*we*—would survive. I became my husband's full-time caregiver—which meant I was in essence a double caregiver, because, with Steve being ill, I was now in sole charge of our autistic daughter. Although Steve underwent conventional treatments, I researched all I could about integrative nutritional therapies and tried some (with the doctor's consent) that were meant to work synergistically with the chemo he was receiving.

Despite our valiant efforts, he succumbed to the cancer a little over seven months after the discovery of the node.

The bad news didn't stop there. Only months after Steve died, my sister's husband was diagnosed with brain cancer. My mother's health declined. My brother-in-law and my mother would both die within the next two years.

The cumulative effect of all that had happened within so short a span of time crushed me. Existence as I had known it was gone. I flatlined emotionally.

I also learned that grief manifests itself in many ways. I wasn't really surprised at the pain—however intense—the panic, the guilt, or even the numbness. What I hadn't known (but was soon to discover) was that grief can wreak havoc on a person's focus. I'd always been an ardent reader and in recent years had been a fairly prolific freelance writer and book reviewer. After Steve died I discovered I couldn't read. The problem wasn't physical or neurological—I had no trouble deciphering letters and words—I simply could not sustain sufficient attention or interest to finish a book, let alone analyze it. Out of a sense of loyalty, I still wrote the occasional review and article for editors with whom I'd had a working relationship over the years. But the effort to produce these pieces was gargantuan, and the results, to my mind, were less than stellar. My heart just wasn't in it anymore—and wouldn't be for a while.

I then recalled several lines in "I Will Survive" that seemed to speak directly to me: *It took all the strength I had not to fall apart,*

Kept trying hard to mend the pieces of my broken heart . . . And I drew inspiration from them.

I knew I'd have to find another path to redefine who I was. I was no longer the bookish writer, just as I was no longer my husband's wife.

My daughter, Jenny, helped to create my psychospiritual makeover. Steve's illness and death had devastated her, but autistic people are famously musical. One evening she surprised me by suggesting we sing together.

"Let's sing a song together to make me feel better inside," she said. So we did, and not just that evening but on subsequent evenings as well. The singing not only helped her to "feel better inside," it helped me too.

My daughter's request awakened memories of a life I had lived before marrying Steve, one in which music played a large role. I used to sing at parties, in small clubs, and in a few local bands. I had even been a busker, singing in the London Tube stations when I was a student in England.

But the responsibilities of marriage and motherhood had overtaken the music. Now I realized how much I'd missed it and how much I wanted it back in my life, not just on the periphery but as a focal point.

I developed children's programs that included a potpourri of stories, folk and fairy tales, and, of course, ghost stories. The programs included a repertoire of songs that crossed cultures, genres, and even languages. I became a familiar figure in schools, churches, and at fairs, singing songs, telling stories, and making children smile.

My new incarnation enabled me to indulge my love of flamboyance, something I'd kept in check (more or less) during the more "reserved" years of my former life. Even small children appreciate bold fashion statements, so my outfits now included sequined and spangled tops, leather pants in every color of the rainbow—plus gold and silver—and an array of boots and hats. (I also bought a new guitar—black—on which I pasted stickers of rhinestone-studded skulls!) The eye-catching attire was the visible representation of my new persona—one with a new vision. I now saw myself as a conveyor of joy, through music and stories, to children. And this vision, in turn, helped to resuscitate and restore my emotional vitality and spiritual balance.

"I Will Survive" continues to be my personal mantra. I often think of certain lyrics in that song, as they closely reflect the battle I waged to overcome the soul-shattering aftermath of widowhood. *At first, I was afraid, I was petrified . . . And I grew strong and I learned how to get along . . .*

I did learn how to get along. I salute Gloria Gaynor for inspiring so many women to move beyond their fears and go forward. As I did.

RECLAIMING MY ROAR
by Mercedes M. Yardley

I'm small town through and through. Born in a rural desert town where you not only know everybody's name, but you know everybody's business. When I took driver's education, the instructor (who also doubled as the football coach and tripled as my classmate's father) taught us to stop at the stop sign and say all four of the town's police officer's names before going again. When somebody's cute cousin came for summer break, everybody was thrilled: fresh meat. Somebody interesting, somebody we hadn't seen through nursery school, through kindergarten, through elementary and middle school. By the time we were old enough to date one another, nobody really wanted to. It's tough to think romantically about the boy whose milk spurted out of his nose in junior high.

I met a guy in college. He also came from a small town. He grew up baling hay and checking on his darling little old neighbors to make sure they were OK. He was the nicest, smartest guy I had ever met. We were married and had a baby. We moved away from our roots, our support system, to the city for graduate school. Moved to a different country for more grad school. We discovered that our baby had a severe genetic disability that affected him in every way possible. Mentally. Physically. It seemed more than I could handle. It wasn't, of course; it became manageable. But at the time? I was floored.

My husband and I have now been married twelve years and have three children. I always thought my life would be full of travel, romance, and finding things that are shiny and exciting and new. That isn't necessarily the case. It's full of other things, such as physical, behavioral, and speech therapies. I have peanut butter on every single item of clothing I own, which are mostly T-shirts and ill-fitting skirts. I also have that frazzled mom hair I swore I'd never have.

My husband is gone more than he is home. He has to be, working hard to support our rambunctious crew. There were supposed to be more of us too. Our youngest was a triplet, but severe anomalies stole the lives of her sisters. We're a house of laughter, but a house of sorrow and pain as well.

At times I feel like I'm not myself. I'm not Mercedes anymore but Mom. The Mother Whose Son Has Williams Syndrome. The Mother Who Lost Her Babies. The Mother Who Always Looks THIS Close to the Edge.

This isn't who I *am*, I think to myself, I'm so much more. There's so much sparkle to my life, or at least there was. But now? The shine has dulled. The shimmer has gone out.

Then I remember this song that I used to dance to wildly when I was in college. Back when I was free and abhorred words like *responsibility* and *for the good of the whole*. I had a little *me*-ness back then and found so much more joy. If I didn't want to do something, well, I didn't always do it. I was free. I was too busy dancing in my room with my friends to Gloria Gaynor's "I Will Survive."

I loved the song so much I participated in a show choir and sang it for my solo. I belted out the part about how it took all the strength I had not to fall apart. The song made me strong. The song had swagger and sparkle, and I borrowed it as my own. I carefully budgeted out the money from one of my five jobs in order to buy a used CD with that song on it. I listened to it nearly every day, several times a day. It got me through scary things: a theater audition (in which I scored the main role) and an extremely painful breakup (which was one of the best decisions I ever made). I learned from Ms. Gaynor's strength and glory and lioness roar when I didn't have that roar myself. The fierceness of her roar carried me.

Now that I'm in my thirties, I have become everything I always feared: a struggling mother whose hair is always up in a bun, whose kids think toast and jam is an acceptable dinner. I feel like I've lost my roar and wonder if Gloria's song can help me like it did when I was eighteen.

I don't see why not. Once a diva, always a diva. Once a powerhouse, always a powerhouse. Gloria's song had enough spunk to pull me through earlier, and that doesn't just die away, does it? No, I don't think so; it simply gets buried somewhere.

I've started making changes. Small ones, in a way. Refusing to drop off my kids at school in my pajama pants. Applying mascara every day, even if only to condition my eyelashes. I've started making bigger changes too. Stepping away from a few of the responsibilities that aren't imperative but are drowning me. I decide to take a month away from social media, even though I'm afraid that I'll lose my writing network and my friends will be hurt by my lack of accessibility. I'm also concerned that my first book, which just came out, will fall into obscurity without promotion and my online presence.

They're small steps. Scary ones. But I press on. I decide to fulfill some of my dreams, including getting involved in some daring activities. I won't put off my dream of going cage diving with great white sharks another five years. I sign up for scuba diving classes so I can get the ball rolling. I even got some help with my kidlets, who are wonderful and amazing and would actually enjoy having a babysitter from time to time.

Most important of all, I have decided to get a master of fine arts degree to make me a better writer. My husband is willing to sacrifice the time and money to make it happen. We're on a spending fast: No more eating out. No more cute crafty things. No more matching dresses for the girls when their wardrobe is already bigger than mine.

Thank you for the sass, Ms. Gaynor—for pulling me through things that seemed serious at the time, and things that seemed nearly dire now. Survival is more than coming back from the insane, crazy situations in which we find ourselves. It also has to do with pulling ourselves out of the abyss of hopelessness, of drudgery, of a life dismal and stressful and without sparkle and shine.

My husband wants a happy wife. My children want a mom who will play with them, who laughs out in the backyard before dinner. These things are happening now that I have my groove back. When I decided I would survive this, that I could turn this song on and again become the woman-child who danced without grace and concern in her little dorm room. I can be that again. I *have* become that again—only it's more fulfilling to dance around when my fantastic, fabulous family is doing it with me.

SOMEHOW

by Lynn Obermoeller

When I married for the second time, I believed with all my heart that this one would be "till death do us part."

We planned to have a large family and, about a year after we married, I gave birth to my first child, a son. Before he turned one, I found out I was pregnant again, with a daughter. Right before her birth, my mother-in-law passed away, and a few months later my father-in-law also died. With all the changes, my husband seemed a little distant—but I felt compassion toward him for having suddenly lost both his parents. We moved into his childhood home, and I continued to make excuses for his behavior: leaving without saying good-bye, lying about where he'd been, coming home late at night.

With the news of my third pregnancy came proof of my husband's affair. All my dreams of a big, happy family vanished. Scared and not knowing what to do or how I would survive on my own with three little babies, I sought counseling from a priest. I convinced my husband to join me, even though neither one of us participated in any kind of religion. In the session my husband claimed he was just "helping this girl."

I wanted to believe him. "If you're helping her, then let me help too. Bring her to the house."

He had promised to protect her from abusive parents and that he wouldn't tell a soul. If I were to help, his promise would be broken. The priest asked, "Even at the cost of your marriage?"

"Yes."

I spiraled into a dark, bottomless pit. I don't remember hearing anything or speaking after that. I called the priest the next day.

"I just want to be clear. Did my husband say that he'd keep his promise to her, even at the cost of our marriage?"

"Well . . . I'm afraid that's what I understood."

"That's what I thought."

The priest explained the benefits of further counseling.

"My husband refuses to go again," I said as I nervously pinched the bridge of my nose.

"You can come by yourself."

Tears ran down my cheek. "What's the point?"

One particular day, full of self-pity and victimhood, I screamed at my four-year-old son and two-year-old daughter as they ran through the house playing. I slammed kitchen drawers and kicked at cabinets. Over my own yells, I heard a different scream come from the family room. *My God, I forgot all about her.* I rushed in and expected to see my four-month-old baby hurt, but she greeted me with a smile. I stood dumbfounded. She screamed again with a beautiful smile on her face. *What could be wrong with her?*

Trying to explain what happened next seems surreal, but my baby and I stared at each other, and I stood transfixed. We communed somehow. It was as if we were actually communicating.

She smiled. I heard her message, not in my ear, but in my mind. "Can you see what you are teaching me?"

"Yes, I see."

"And is this what you want to teach me?"

"No."

"So, what are you going to do about it?"

"I don't know. I guess something will have to change. But what? What am I supposed to do? Your daddy lies about everything. He pretends to *help* this girl. I can't even call her a woman. She's so young. Just out of high school. He's having an affair with her. I cry every day. I barely eat. I hardly sleep. I drag myself out of bed. What had gone wrong? What did I do? Wasn't I a good wife and mother?

Wasn't this what we'd planned? To have a family and live happily ever after?"

How could I describe to my baby the emptiness in my heart or my thoughts of slitting my wrists or taking a bottle of pills? I wanted to explain everything that ran through my head.

But it wasn't necessary. She understood my anger and pain, my hurt and confusion. She understood it all. Somehow.

Her eyes twinkled. She smiled at me. "And . . .? What are you going to do?" Her silent voice echoed in my heart.

And I knew.

I knew right then that the change would have to come from me. I had choices. The ache resurfaced. I was afraid. I questioned everything. *How am I going to make money? Where will we live? What will happen to us? Will uprooting the kids be the right thing? What if this is a mistake? How will I manage this all on my own? How am I . . .*

I stopped myself. A deep, inner calling beckoned . . . and I remembered the words to Gloria Gaynor's song. I felt her words: I was petrified. Then her refrain became my mantra, *I will survive.* Somehow.

I pulled on an inner strength—it was as if I had become unstuck. The angry, feel-sorry-for-me attitude turned to future dreams. A new home for my three children and myself. Setting a different example. Happiness. Teaching my children about love. Real love.

We moved out three months later and started anew. Eventually I remarried, for a third time. After two years that marriage came to an end too.

Single once more with my three little ones, I felt like a complete failure. I saw the way people looked at me when I shared with them that I was getting a divorce . . . for the *third* time. I overheard comments about the number of my marriages.

I was surviving, but there was something missing. I dug deeper to understand myself. I discovered I wasn't a failure. I'd just made poor choices when it came to men because I lacked confidence and self-esteem.

This revelation became clear to me one day while I was kneeling in the yard digging up weeds. A neighbor came over to thank me for watching her little girl one rainy night several weeks before.

I had heard screaming at my back door, and when I opened it, her barefoot little girl sobbed, "My daddy is trying to kill my mommy!" I pulled her in and immediately called 911. Her daddy was taken to jail, but his parents bailed him out. My neighbor apologized and told me she had been embarrassed to face me sooner.

I pulled more weeds while the little girl's mother continued to talk. "What can I do? I mean, I'm stuck. I have three kids."

I didn't utter a word. I knew exactly what she was going through. I understood the humiliation of having cop cars pull up to your house. I also knew she'd have to figure out when she'd had enough. She'd come to the realization that she'd survive—without abuse—when she was ready. She spoke again: "Yeah, look at what I'm saying . . . you're doing it, aren't you?"

My breath caught hold. Yes, I was doing it! Leaving each husband was no cakewalk, but I'd discovered sweetness like no other. I realized how courageous it was for me to leave rather than stay in an abusive relationship. There was always something good to come out of each experience. Self-discovery, three beautiful children, getting off the merry-go-round of alcoholism. More discoveries than I could have imagined. I knew how to stay alive. And more.

I had a lot of love to give . . . and I fell in love again and married for a fourth time, to a wonderful man.

Regardless of what obstacles I may face, what pain I may have to endure, or what hardship may be in store for me . . . there is no doubt I will survive, somehow.

WHAT IF I DIDN'T WANT
TO SURVIVE?

by Sue Carswell

In August 2005, Hurricane Katrina happened. I was devastated by the images I saw on television of people being lifted off their roofs by helicopters, screaming and begging to be saved after the failed levies wreaked hell, when it seemed God simply shut his eyes.

When I was young, I was the one who'd pet the animals in the fields—of the first backyard I grew up in—before they were slaughtered. And then, when we moved to my second backyard—the grounds of an orphanage—I was the one who'd smile at the orphans, who walked around as if tranquilized and in a trance.

That's how I knew I could be of service in New Orleans, if only to lend a shoulder to cry on. I decided to use my vacation to go there to help. Prior to my trip, I completed thirty hours of disaster relief training with the Red Cross in order to become a client services volunteer. It would be my job to welcome residents back to their homes—or what was left of their homes. It seemed like a place where I belonged.

When I arrived in New Orleans, it became clear immediately that most of the houses were gone. Mattresses and tricycles were wrapped around majestic elms. A ripped American flag flapped in the mid-October breeze. During the days that followed, I listened to dozens of stories of how people had fled. Some had run; some were evacuated by helicopters; others drove. All of them thought, I will survive . . .

My experience as a reporter, book editor, and TV news producer helped people feel safe in opening up to me about the tragedies they'd experienced. One ex-prisoner I spoke to told me he'd been stuck on a bridge, chained together with other inmates, as the water rose all around him. Another man cried, "I wanted to save my cats but couldn't," and showed me water-stained pictures of his destroyed home. I'd imagined that immersing myself in these people's stories would erase my own morbid sadness. But there were just so *many* of these stories, each more devastating than the last: "I stayed until the looters came" . . . "I lost my wife" . . . "I lost my daughter" . . . "I don't know if I can carry on" . . . "I don't know if I have the will to live anymore . . ." By the end of my "vacation," I felt fried. I needed to flee all the suffering before *I* collapsed. In essence, as Gloria Gaynor sings, *I was petrified* . . .

But the damage was done: when I returned home, my trip triggered a depression like nothing I'd ever experienced. I sat in my living room for hours, holding my head in my hands. These were my thoughts: Should I jump in front of a subway or leap from the open window I'd pried the nails off long ago? Would a four-story fall kill me or merely leave me with broken bones? There were also the pills in my medicine cabinet, which would allow me to sleep my life away . . .

The next day at work it became clear I'd reached the point where a simple visit to my psychiatrist's office could no longer cure me. I was suicidal, mere steps away from ending my life. I reached out to a friend at *Vanity Fair*, who spoke to my psychiatrist. Later that afternoon I agreed to check myself into a psychiatric ward at NYU Medical Center. My doctor made me promise to take a taxi, as subways are vehicles for suicide. For the first time I felt a tiny glimmer of relief: Help was only a taxi ride away, and I couldn't wait to get it. I've always believed you can't get to heaven if you end your own life. Although I longed to be by my mother's side, I knew I had to choose life.

In the cab I started crying hysterically. How long would I have to stay in the hospital? A week? A month? Longer? Would the ward be full of people worse off than I, run by a Nurse Ratched? The unknowns were terrifying. Would they finally diagnose exactly what it was that was wrong with me? When I arrived, I signed a form with a quivering hand, near the statement that said I was willing to stay in the psych ward until the doctors agreed to let me go. I was put into a wheelchair, and a nurse asked to see my bag. She took away my Advil, which posed a risk of overdose. She took my pens, which she said were too sharp to keep. Then she took my mother's precious Mikimoto pearls, which were deemed a "harmful threat"—something I could strangle myself with, I suppose. Feeling as if the nurse was taking away a piece of my mother, I started to protest, but the medication I'd been given was kicking in; drifting away from the nurse's rapid-fire questions, I fell asleep in my wheelchair.

The next morning, I walked to the cafeteria in blue hospital pants and a shirt. I ate cornflakes and cut up my banana with a fork, as knives—even plastic ones—weren't allowed. Once I resigned myself to the fact that I was staying, I started to relax a bit. After breakfast, our activities director handed out coloring books. I couldn't believe that I—then a forty-three-year-old woman—was being asked to color. But somehow the simple task was soothing. An old lady with no teeth sat next to me, humming, as she crayoned an orange Cinderella. In many ways coloring made me feel young again, like I was starting anew. It was like being in kindergarten, and I knew I would have to get through all the grades in order to graduate out of the psych ward.

Group therapy sessions began the next day. I sat in a room with a psychiatrist and seven other patients. Our reasons for being there were as diverse as my former backyard full of orphans and sick children. We talked about feelings. That was the question posed to us: "What *are* feelings?" Some people didn't know what the psychiatrist meant. I simply said, "They're located where the heart is." We talked about sadness. It was all very simple. "What is sadness?" the psychiatrist asked . . . I thought to myself, sadness is a snapshot of my group. Sadness is my life. Then the therapist turned to me and said, "Tell me about your childhood." I talked about the profound effect the orphans had had on me, how watching them navigate their lost childhoods had sent me into a tailspin of obsession that I would lose mine. I talked about how that feeling only grew stronger as I grew older—and how, once I *did* lose my mother, I'd been unable to really grieve, instead holding it all in and just feeling irritated all the time, crying only when I overheard other people's sad stories.

"Were you close to your mother?" the therapist asked.

"She was my world," I replied. "Nothing since she left has ever really mattered to me."

And suddenly, for whatever reason, I started to cry. I cried for my mother and for all the years I had kept in those deep feelings of grief. I was in a safe place. In the psych ward I no longer had to be at the top of my game. No one had any expectations of me. I was the one who had to pull myself back together and rebuild part of my soul, even finding a place to cry about the loss of my mother.

Over the next few days, I got involved in my ward, challenging a young Hasidic boy named Sammy to a game of Ping-Pong. I began to feel hopeful. For the first time, I was diagnosed as bipolar, and that was incredibly eye-opening. I had been put on a bipolar drug before, but because I felt too drugged on it, I was immediately taken off of it. This time I was given a drug named ABILIFY. Again I felt tranquilized and not right. Instead of pulling me off the drug, they adjusted my dose. Slowly, through my stay on the psych ward, I started feeling better than I had ever felt before. Had I been misdiagnosed all these years? Since there was no sense blaming anyone, I just accepted my new medication and was grateful that something was making me start to feel what I imagined "normal" felt like. I had never felt normal before. Not even as a kid, so I had nothing to compare it to. But little by little I felt the sadness and despair start to evaporate, even among this community of deeply disturbed people. I began to feel like I would survive.

Eight days after I was admitted, I was cleared to leave. I packed up my belongings, including a birdcage I had made, and even beaded bracelets, and walked out the front door with my dad and back into the world—a place I'd found so unforgiving for so long. The difference was that I now knew that, if I fell down again in the future, I had a haven to return to. If the bipolar medication needed further adjustment, I had faith that my psychiatrist could handle it. I just needed to be open and always tell her how I was feeling, and not let time pass and darker feelings fester. For the first time in a long time, I felt safe. Once again I was wearing my mother's pearls as my father and I made our way to my apartment. The pearls completed me—they were my mother's love wrapped around my neck.

THE CRACK HEARD AROUND THE WORLD

by Michael Gabriel

The year was 1971—right away you think to yourself, *Oh, that was a long time ago.* But for me, in my mind, it was just a moment ago. I was six and a half years old, not yet at the age of knowledge, still truly innocent. Television was not full of sex back then. There was no Internet, and porn was still in its infancy. Being raised on a farm in rural Virginia, all I knew was fishing, playing tag with my friends in the cool evenings after church as the parents talked, and spending time with my loving family. My parents were not savvy to the evils of the world—a mistake I hated them for, for many years to come. The trauma I went through was different than that of a woman being raped or someone having his best friend blown up right next to him in war. In adulthood you know the risk of something like the aforementioned happening. My experience was not better or worse, just different.

It began with a man my family had met through our church. His name was Dallas. He lived with his mother, a sweet, elderly woman who was a pillar in our Baptist church. He was divorced and a bit odd by today's standards. The friendship with my family started when he asked my father to keep some cattle for him on our farm. He came by pretty often to check on his livestock and tinker around our house doing odds and ends, things my dad had no time for. As Dallas and my father grew in friendship, we saw more and more of him and his mother. One day, for no reason I can remember, Dallas asked if I could sleep over at his house to spend time with him and his mother. At the young age of six, I was happy to get some attention from a male figure, since Dad always worked, and my only playmates were my two sisters. My parents said, "Sure, why not?" So for the next few months, at least one Saturday a month, I stayed at Dallas and his mother's home. We ate ice cream, watched scary movies on television, and I slept next to Dallas in his room. Sometimes he would rub his penis up against me or ask me to rub it through his pajamas. Truly, I thought nothing of it. It seemed strange, but being innocent and six, I knew nothing else, so I thought it was normal.

All that changed the day my family and I went on a fishing trip with my father's other best friend, George. Both George and Dallas were about forty-five years of age, but George was a family man, with kids of his own, and the most successful business owner we knew. He owned a lakeside cabin and a fishing cruiser. I was very excited we were going, since I had never been on a boat. As far as I could tell, Dallas and George had only one thing in common, *me*.

My family and I made the two-hour trip to George's cabin. It was a warm spring day full of sunshine, blue skies, and dark blue water. My father caught the first fish of the day, and we all had a great time. Back at the cabin, after dinner, George asked if I could stay behind to spend the night and fish the next day with him and some friends who would come down in the morning. My parents said, "Sure, why not?" After they left, we had ice cream, watched television, and then he suggested that I sleep in his room. As with Dallas, he began to rub himself on me, but then things suddenly changed. He exposed his penis and asked me to rub it for him. This was scary for me because Dallas had never exposed himself to me.

I remember thinking to myself, *my parents trust Mr. George; he is our friend, so I guess this is normal.* I did what he asked me to do, but there was a dark feeling in the room. When he climaxed I was taken aback by the emission; it seemed gross and frightening. Then he said to me, "You can lick it off if you want. That's what the girls do."

That's what the girls do?

With that statement, my brain thundered and cracked like every gun in the world had just gone off all at once. My innocence, my childhood, my faith, my happiness, my trust, ran down my face and onto the floor, never to be seen or enjoyed again. I was being used. I was being used as a woman. I must not be normal. This was not normal. It was wrong. Unable to think, unable to accept what was happening, my cracked mind shut down, just as if it had been split open by a steel bat. Not able to talk, crying uncontrollably, he placed me in the spare room in the hope, I guess, that I would sleep off my tears. The next day only snapshots remained in my mind.

On the boat, fishing with George and his other friends, I laid curled up in a fetal position, whimpering. He made an offhanded remark to the others that I was homesick. On the way back home, curled up in the backseat, still crying silently, he gave me a warning: If I told anyone of our secret, our family Boston terrier, Tina, would be killed.

That's it. That is what I recall from the day that changed my life forever. For the next three months I told no one. Anger ruled my life. The happy child gone, replaced by a monster who at seven years old bloodied his sister's fourteen-year-old boyfriend because he teased him. Blackouts of rage became my new normal.

As time passed I could take the secret and anger no more. One afternoon, as my mother sat on our front porch, I told her the whole story. She cried and had me recite the story to my father and his sister, who was there at the time. I expected my father to rise to my defense. I expected him to take up my war cry and show these men that I had a father who was a lion and the champion of his children. But once again I was betrayed. After an hour of shock and awe from all three listeners, my father decided that if he confronted them, he might kill them and end up in jail. He sat there and rationalized that pressing charges, involving the courts, would not undo what had happened to me. How shameful if this got out, his two best friends molesting his seven-year-old son. So it was decided that they would do nothing. No confrontation, no police involvement, no courts. Nothing.

It took nearly four months for me to raise the courage to tell this nasty, degrading story. Four months of fear. Four months of hatred. Four months of nightmares—and for what? Only to find out my father was *not* my protector. I was truly alone in this world. Sadness and hatred were now my constant companions. Thoughts of suicide were ever close, and the next two years were full of depression, missed days of school, and self-loathing.

My parents' response to my rage and sadness was to send me to a lowbrow, free counseling center. Not one of the counselors ever suggested going after the predators. There were no insights or suggestions on how to cope whatsoever. Now I am nine, and the next big question searing my brain is . . . *am I gay?*

I did not feel an attraction to boys, yet if two different men used me for sex, they must be gay, right? So if they sought me out, they must have seen something in me that was gay, right? So am I gay or not? What will my life be like if I can never be "normal"? Will every day be more of the same: guilt, depression, self-loathing? Why go on? I think by now you can understand the black sea of soup I was swimming in.

Many people say I am on the road to recovery, or that I am picking up where I left off. Those who have experienced similar situations to mine can understand this. You can come back from physical injuries, but my road was destroyed; in one second I went from childhood to adulthood, and I had to find a new path. At ten years of age, the pastor at our church read the scripture that states, "Unless you forgive you cannot be forgiven," so I began to forgive and ask God for forgiveness. But this did not change the sexual questions I had for myself. That answer to my sexuality came in the form of a girl—a girl who was also sexually abused by two family members at a very young age. My sister's best friend and I began a secret relationship that lasted until I was in ninth grade and she was almost a senior in high school. She was almost four years older than me, and I loved her with my heart, body, and soul. Religion and sex are noncompatible components in America, but I needed both for my mental survival.

I forgave Dallas and George but will never forget what they did to me. I also forgive my parents for their lack of diligence, support, and protection when I needed it most. Through the relationship with my sister's friend, I discovered my true sexual identity and my love for females. To this foundation I added twelve years of martial arts, guitar, and a master's in theology; I became a regional director of Jos. A. Bank, which specializes in high-end apparel for men, a bank manager, and now have my own business. This is not my résumé— it's what I paved my own road with. My wife and children benefit from my experiences. I am a protective father, and I do not allow sleepovers. I spend time with my son and daughter and protect them like the lion I have become. Like Ms. Gloria Gaynor's song "I Will Survive," I have survived and thrived, yet the scars never disappeared, and even now as I write this, I feel the wet drops of what was stolen from me grace my face once more.

THE BLACK EYE OF THE STORM

by Juliette Summers

Take a deep breath and lie as still as you possibly can," said the X-ray technician from behind the protective glass enclosure. I lay there battling my tear ducts on a surface as hard as my husband's heart. I silently opened Heaven's door, like a child creeping into his parents' bedroom seeking comfort, and brought my shattered dreams to God as the large equipment slowly moved over my injuries. Like God asking Adam in the Garden of Eden, I posed the same question to myself: "Where are you?"

What was I doing here and how did this happen? I shuddered briefly and corrected myself so the X-ray wouldn't blur. My husband's mask was much larger than it had appeared and fell hard after our nuptials, less than a year earlier. This wasn't my first injury by his hand. I'd already earned several stripes on my marital uniform's sleeve. I'd even driven myself, in spite of the broken bones in my right foot, to the emergency room that night, as the offending party refused to help me gain treatment.

As I was littered with multiple contusions and Technicolor bruises, the technician helped me into a wheelchair and elevated my swollen, purple foot. Turning, she said, "The doctor will be with you shortly, and your husband just arrived." My husband *just* arrived. Glancing at my watch, I confirmed that three hours had passed since I'd first arrived.

A young doctor approached with my films in his hand. I offered a lopsided smile due to facial swelling. Oddly, I wanted to offer reassurance that things were all right. It wasn't my first visit to an emergency room with similar injuries, nor would it be my last. But this doctor saw behind the flesh and bone he'd studied in medical school and quickly located the deepest wound.

"I know what *really* happened tonight," he said. "I can help you. Get you to a safe place again."

Shocked and embarrassed by his perception, I quickly went into "Christianese" and began faithfully covering up my husband's sin, a duty I felt I was obligated to by my marital vows.

The doctor dismissed my answers and again offered help, stating he'd already seen my husband but was withholding his professional evaluation. I hesitated, silently calculating the result should the truth emerge. No, I decided. The situation was too volatile. Besides, I am a Christian whose love has to forgive a multitude of sins. I pretended not to comprehend the doctor's offer. It was a decision I would live to regret.

After the incident I was again locked out of the bedroom and not allowed to sleep in our bed for days, while he explained my "accident" to family and friends. It was always the same: utter denial coupled with a complete lack of empathy.

As I lay in the dark on the sofa with a battered, throbbing body and elevated broken toes, I found myself asking the same question over and over through burning tears: "Lord, don't *you* care?" While my husband snored blissfully in his soft bed, I collected my thoughts into a tangled pile, then, throughout the night, I separated and sorted them until things seemed organized. With a few more adjustments and calibrations, I came to the hard truth: *My husband had no intention of changing.* He was content with the status quo and believed me to be the real problem.

The reality hit hard, far exceeding the pain of my physical assault. The latest beating forced me to soberly evaluate my future with him. It would only continue if something didn't interrupt his abusive, erratic patterns. Likewise, it appeared that the only possible change on the horizon would be mine. I chose to pray for him to love our children and me, and hope that intervention could refocus his violent choices.

And so I resolved to seek counseling for our marriage rather than put the children through some judicial trauma. In an unexpected flashback to being single and carefree, the distant echo in my memory grew louder and clearer until the words were pristine. I seized assurance, strength, and courage from Gloria Gaynor's storied declaration back when disco was king, bell-bottoms were must-haves, and flashing lights were all the rage. Closing my eyes, I could see her belting out that song under bright lights and calling the downtrodden to rise up and love themselves. Once again, she gave me my song in the night. With hope renewed and a rare smile, I drifted into restless sleep.

And I grew strong and I learned how to get along . . .

Years clicked by like the meter in a taxicab. I silently watched my mate as his gossamer ethics eroded still further. Brass rings are deceptive when hollow victories are sought. A new job presented a move and a fresh start. Unbeknownst to me, God was lining up my exodus with that employment offer. Despite the inexhaustible antagonism at home, God proved himself faithful. He steadfastly continued to answer prayers as I chose to stay anchored by his divine side. I persevered in growth as he prepared me for the future and poured an immovable foundation beneath me.

The dream I sold myself with our new start proved to be futile. Genuine change must be wanted and sought, with the willingness to make sacrifices for each other. With the addition of another child, my "accidents" increased, as did my permanent injuries. Exhausted from fruitless counseling, my reality had come full circle. There were no figs on this tree, and I couldn't deny the truth any longer. Too many lives were at stake. Once again, I waited for an emergency-room doctor to explain my injuries. The physical freedoms I'd previously enjoyed had now been stolen by immobility and chronic pain. This time, when the doctor asked how I had come to have such precision-placed blows, I broke my silence after eight agonizing years and baptized both of us with my tears. He was keenly aware of the emotional mask shrouding a battered spouse and commended my courage. Knowing the routine, I again hobbled home to the sofa.

Was this phase of my walk an easy journey? No. My husband continued to actively batter me. His anger left permanent damage to my body. There were more doctors and emergency-room visits. More X-rays, injections, braces, prescriptions, physical therapy, insurance claims, and failed interventions. It appeared I was accident-prone, though my accidents were tightly confined to the parameters of the marriage.

With this new epiphany, I dove deep. I reached up for God and He reached down to me. I immediately discovered the Lord couldn't resist the words "Teach me." He did. Our odyssey has continued uninterrupted all these years. Even though I had children and the terrors of a hostile marriage, He brought balance, direction, and protection to my life.

I took every avenue to prevent the inevitable. Finally, with numerous marriage counselors asking me, "Why are you staying in this violent marriage?" I grasped my freedom and permanently fled the unhealthy union. I had to wrestle the gorilla of free will and accept that I couldn't be responsible for another's actions or choices. It had taken years for me to arrive at this destination, realizing God supported my decision for safety—even though my nature still made me want to salvage my marital vows. I subsequently learned it takes two spouses to actively invest in a happy marriage.

We all face areas we cannot control. We can run circles exhausting ourselves, apply ineffective salves, blame God, or wholly trust him to ride out the storm. Sadly, many women in my former situation haven't yet discovered their priceless value because it's constantly been eroded by the very one with whom they've chosen to share their lives. Too often, sadly, their lives are extinguished.

When Christ healed the ten lepers, it is documented, they were "healed as they went." In other words, there was no evidence of health *until* they embarked on their journey. I, too, experienced progressive healing with every step I took *away* from bondage until finally

I was whole again. Who would have guessed that I would be healed by Gloria Gaynor—an up-and-coming singer from New Jersey who was, in fact, an undercover physician and counselor, mending my heart and restoring my emotions? Believing the famous lyrics this songstress wove into the fabric of my life, I can now sing them with personal conviction.

My courageous Disco Doctor has gratefully and passionately taught me . . . *I will survive*!

WAYWARD CELLS

by Jean Knight Pace

Everyone's mother is dead or dying. It is nothing new, nothing ceasing, nothing fresh or interesting. But when *your* mother is dying, you feel her bones in your own, and that insistence stretches into the vision you have of your own life.

My mother hobbles from her condo to the pool. Her key is attached to a bracelet on her wrist. Her hair is mostly gone on one side of her head. Her skin is warm but loose. She insists on speech, but none of it comes out in the way she intends. To compensate, I ramble on about the things in our life—the kids, the ducks, the house. And my children swirl like bees, eager to swim, to vacation with Grandma, to run up the stairs of the condo. They love the wigs she rarely bothers to wear anymore, the cane that rests by her door. They love sick Grandma as much as whole Grandma. In fact, I'm not really sure they're aware of the difference.

Sometimes I envy them, because I feel the difference acutely. On this trip I feel it more than usual and realize that through our weekly phone calls Mom has concealed much of her decline from me. Or perhaps it has just come up on her in a rush as the tumor in the side of her brain crowds out the woman who is my mother.

My mother and I have always been close. Not in the girly ways some women connect. We have never once done one another's nails, or even considered it. We have shopped together only out of necessity and with the pragmatic efficiency of small-town women for whom the mall is an hour away.

But I have always been a good talker, and she has always had an open ear. It made for a good match. In my almost completely innocent days of high school and college, I told her nearly everything. Back then, in her faithful looking to bright-future-day days, she listened and even told me some things about her own life, which, for my mother, was not the type of thing that poured out with ease.

Now I talk of weather, of treatments, of complicated drug names. My mother, meanwhile, sits by the pool—a stone wall bleached white by the sun.

Her future is to be cut short, her present a confusing and uncomfortable place in which to stand, and her past shadowed a bit too darkly by cloudy days for her to well remember the achingly sunny ones.

As if in cruel punishment for her complaints, the tumor in her brain winds into her speech—verbs, tenses, and rules of grammar once so carefully observed are cast aside by the tentacles of wayward cells. Her word order changes, as though translated by a computer from a foreign tongue. And thoughts my mother is quite lucid enough to think refuse to take shape into clauses and participles, vowels and consonants lined up properly into the words she does utter.

In the weeks just before my arrival in Utah, phone conversation became difficult, almost impossible. We cut it off as gracefully as we could when Mom's words crumbled into a heap I could not properly assemble.

Now, here with her, sitting together on her porch on an overcast evening—my husband and children engaged in a game of hide and seek—the silences and disconnects do not weigh so much, and we can enjoy each other a bit more, as mother and daughter should. Yet I have this face-to-face camaraderie for only a few worrisome days before I fly back over state after state, and the phone—while she can still operate it—becomes our only recourse.

And all the while, I continue to die too—not in the solid way of a woman harboring a brain tumor, but in the way that we are all dying— slowly, surely, and mostly imperceptibly. Here in my midthirties, watching my mother decline, it seems much more palpable than it did fifteen years ago. Now it's easier to see the way my brain refuses to find a word it knows it knows, or to put that word in the right place when I'm tired, easier to see the forced quiet that this could eventually become.

To watch thirty/forty/fiftysomething actresses with their clever television quips, their careers laid out in the steely feminism that promises protection from dependence and decline, their breasts and faces propped up with plastic and creams and lasered invasions. To see these women is not to think of dying. To see these women is to see a careful scaffold built against age itself. Instead, I remember and cling to the words of the song . . . *I've got all my life to live, and I've got all my love to give, and I'll survive.*

To hold my mother's hand—a hand that used to be as solid and strong as eternity, and to feel the skin soft and thin, to feel the lack of muscle one does not realize a hand possesses until it is gone, to know that the control and use of that hand is now limited by the erratic waves neurally transmitted to it. To see this is to see the ashes I will become.

And while I, of a religious nature, do not inherently fear ash or dust, it's easier to accept with calmness and patience when it belongs to an unrelated someone's life cycle.

I cannot do the "warm-up" Sudoku puzzle I hold in my lap. I feel I must master it before the plane ride home ends—must reassure myself that the synapses are still firing and connecting. But when, near the end, two sevens blink at me from the same row, I scratch a heavy line through it and we land.

My mother calls to see if we returned safely. Her words line up correctly, and I tell her that we have. I might as well stand up and sing, "I will survive . . . " because knowing she can still call me on the phone does something for me. And looking at my family reminds me that as the song says, "As long as I know how to love, I know I'll stay alive," in their hearts, as my mother will in mine.

The next day I steal my nine-year-old's Sudoku book and work for forty-five minutes on the one titled "very easy." It's well past my bedtime when I conquer it, but I feel a small tinge of relief. There is still life left to grab. For me, and in these last precious months, for her.

WE THREE

by Andrea Harris

From outside the bedroom door his profanities grow louder, so I begin to sing a little stronger: *As long as I know how to love, I know I'll stay alive . . .*

My three-year-old snuggles under the covers of his bed as I gently rub his back. When the yelling finally stops and my child in the bed is asleep, I continue softly singing, for myself and my baby yet to be born. I am worried about the little one inside me. The doctors have diagnosed intrauterine growth retardation: the healthy food I eat is not making its way to him. I can tell by the doctor's face that there is reason for concern.

We are living on a US military base overseas, far from my family. I have been married less than a year and feel very much alone. The idea of leaving the country had seemed romantic and freeing when my husband had first proposed to me. I had been raped the year before, and both the healing and the legal processes had been exhausting. Although the man who raped me had been put in prison, reminders of the pain were everywhere I turned. The soft-spoken soldier who told me he wanted to take care of me and my son had seemed like a way out, a refuge. And now I sit here singing softly to my two boys, wondering if we three will survive.

I am singing to myself in my hospital bed. At least I think I'm singing. I am weak from the strain on my pregnant body, and I am groggy from the drugs being pumped into me to prevent my baby from coming too early. I am singing to drown out the rushing of the fears in my head. I cannot lose this baby. I want the words of the song to block the ugly, horrifying words of the doctor: words like "lungs not developed" and "won't survive if born now." I am reliving that pause before he answered my question about the potential side effects of the drugs they were giving me. I am wracked with guilt—over my body's failure to nourish and protect my unborn child, and over my awareness that as I lie here in this hospital bed my older son is alone with his stepfather. I feel as though I have failed both my children, but there is nothing I can do except lie still and accept the drugs. If I don't, my baby will be born too early to survive. So I must stay here in this hospital bed and sing for our survival. I try to make the words come out strong, and I pray that my singing somehow finds its way to the sick little boy inside me and to my scared little boy at home.

Two years later, back in the United States, my husband is packing to leave, and I am sitting at the kitchen table, explaining to my now five-year-old son that his stepfather will be leaving and won't ever be coming back. He is relieved, but he is also worried about how we will make it on our own. He pats my hand and says, "Don't worry, Mommy. I'll help take care of us." His little brother, now two years old, is babbling incoherently to himself, in what we have come to call his "alien language." I have no idea if my younger son has heard what I have just said about his father, no idea if he even recognizes the man in our home as his father. We are on a waiting list to see a doctor who specializes in autism-spectrum disorders. My son has yet to say a single coherent word or syllable—not even a "Mama" or "Dada." He reacts negatively to most human contact, actively resists my touch, and does not respond at all to human voices, including my own. I am terrified that my son will never know me as his mother, will never hug me or say my name. After I put the boys to bed, I sit back down wearily at the table and wonder how I will pay the bills, how we will survive—just us three.

I smile when I hear the words *I Will Survive* on the radio. I turn up the volume, just a little, because my son gets upset when the music is too loud. He is staring out the window from his car seat. We are on our way to the center for kids with developmental issues, where he is receiving occupational and speech therapies. The people at the center are wonderful, but I dread going because it is always a stark reminder of my fears for my son. Since three-year-olds aren't yet adept with language or known for their social or communication skills, my son's condition is not yet obvious. But at the center, as I look around at all the older children, who are so obviously different from "normal" children, I feel panic rise within me. I recognize that the other families love the center because it is one of the few places they can go where they fit in, where they are welcomed without stares or pity. I do not want that life for my son. I turn up the volume of the song on the radio just a bit and begin to sing along. When I glance at my son in the rearview mirror, I see he has turned his face away from the window and is staring at me, smiling ever so slightly. I dare to hope that he recognizes the words I am singing to him.

One night ten years later, I hear the familiar music coming from my younger son's room, and I struggle to get out of bed, my movement largely enabled by pain medication. A car accident had dislocated my hip and traumatized my back, which was already weakened by disc degeneration. I move so slowly that I am afraid I won't make it to my son's room before the song has ended. At thirteen, he talks nonstop, so much so that his older brother and I often ask each other, "Remember when he didn't say a word?" Of course, neither of us would ever exchange his constant prattling of scientific facts with silence. He likes music but is embarrassed to sing or dance in public. With his bedroom door shut, he will dance and sing exuberantly, but if anyone opens the door he will stop. Today, though, I need to see my son dancing. The doctor had told me that I was lucky to be alive, and every day since I returned home from the hospital in a wheelchair, my younger son has made me promise him that I will not die. So now, having survived once again, I need to see him dancing and singing to the song I sang to him when he was still inside me. He is on the last chorus when I finally make it to his door. I crack it open just enough to watch him.

"Mom, what are you doing up?" he asks me worriedly.

"I wanted to see you dance," I tell him.

"Oh. OK."

He moves toward his computer to start the music over but then comes to the doorway and stops just a few inches in front of me. It's the way he tells me that he wants a hug. As he stands perfectly still, I gently hug him. Then I ask him to play the song again so I can sing along. Together we sing as he dances wildly around the room in crazed robot fashion. We are belting out "I Will Survive" when my older son comes out of his room across the hall. He takes one look at the two of us and rolls his eyes, as only teenagers can, but I hear him softly singing to himself as he goes back into his room.

We have survived, we three.

HUMMING THE SONG

by Oxsana Naumkin

We live on a peaceful, small cul-de-sac in Saratoga Springs, New York. We moved there from Brooklyn, New York, six years ago—my husband, Yuri, and my two beautiful sons, Nicholas, nine, and Peter, four—just a few minutes away from my parents, Nina and Oleg Moston. We headed to upstate New York to get away from the hustle and bustle of the big city, and to live someplace beautiful and tree-lined. We were very happy in our new home; never in a million years could we imagine that the biggest tragedy of our lives was lurking just around the corner and that our lives would be forever changed.

Our older son, Nicholas—or Kolya, as we called him—was a handsome, smart, witty boy who loved music, dance, theater, reading, and, of course, video games. Nicholas was a fantastic big brother who took wonderful care of Peter, who is a special child. He was a wonderful friend. He always stood up for kids who were being bullied and made efforts to reach out to new kids who hadn't made any friends yet and felt out of place. He was bilingual and dreamed of studying journalism at the Moscow University. My son was very proud of his Russian heritage.

On December 22, 2010, he came home from school; it was the last day before winter break and just three days before Christmas. One of his classmates called and asked if he would like to come for a sleepover, and Nicholas happily accepted. When I got home from work and realized that he had forgotten his antibiotic, which had been prescribed a day earlier, my husband Yuri decided to drive it over to him. About fifteen minutes later, I received a call from my husband that no parent ever wants to get. His voice sounded strange as he explained that he was in a police car headed to Albany Medical Center, where Nicholas was taken after having been shot by his friend. He said he didn't know the extent of the injury but thought that Nicholas was shot in the head, because the police wouldn't release any details.

I felt faint and nauseated but had to get myself together quickly. I called my friends, Tom and Mary, and asked for help. Mary took Peter, while Tom drove me to the hospital, telling me the entire way not to worry—everything would be OK. When we got to the hospital, the doctor came out and said that Kolya was shot in the head and that the CAT scan didn't show any brain activity. Just like that, in a split second, our beautiful, precious son was *gone*. We felt numb and in complete shock and disbelief.

The devastating news of Nicholas's death stunned the entire community. Christmas Eve was a blur as neighbors gathered outside our home, letting out tears and sobs of rage and singing "Silent Night" amid lit white candles. How could a gun be so carelessly left unsecured by a parent? How could two twelve-year-old boys be left alone with it in the house? How could his friend point the gun at Nicholas's head as a joke and pull the trigger, thinking that the gun was not loaded? I am sure everyone wondered how we would be able to survive this. How could any of us go on? It took all the strength I had not to fall apart.

We come from a very artistic and musical family. Yuri and my mom, Nina, are professional actors. My brother Maxim is a violinist and his wife, Alexandra, is an oboist, both in Broadway musicals. At Kolya's wake they played beautiful music accompanied by my dad, a pianist, while hundreds of visitors sat in silence in the church and cried.

We buried Nicholas on a cold and snowy December day. Burying a child is something that no parent should ever have to endure. It is the most painful and cruel thing you could ever imagine.

On New Year's Eve, the ninth day after Nicholas's passing (a very important day in the Russian Orthodox faith), we came home from the cemetery. It was surreal. Everyone clung together to survive the unbearable pain. We repeatedly watched a video of Nicholas playing the leading role of Baloo in his fifth-grade drama club production of *The Jungle Book*. We chuckled a bit while watching because his bear costume had come undone, and he had to hold it up to prevent it from falling while managing to flawlessly play his part, sing, and dance. Was it possible to survive the agony of such loss?

Music played an important part in our lives, especially now. My dad always tried to make everyone feel better, as he had done in the past. He sat down at the piano that night and began playing—softly at first, but before we knew it everyone began to sing. There were a lot of tears and hugging and holding of hands. Thank God for my father.

On the frigid evening of January 3, 2011, my mom and dad went to visit Nicholas's grave. They weren't drivers, so they went by bus and walked to the cemetery. After spending some time there, my grief-stricken parents started walking back in silence. At some point my mom turned her head to see if Dad was behind her, but he wasn't there. She saw him walking in the opposite direction. She called to him, but he didn't respond, continuing to walk into the darkness toward a busy road that is connected to the highway. Eyewitnesses said that Dad wasn't responsive to anyone or anything and that he kept walking down the ramp to the highway, which he tried to cross. He was struck by a tractor trailer and killed instantly. My dad, who had played such a beautiful tribute to his grandson just four days before, was now tragically taken from this world and from his family in a split second.

Three years have passed. Not a day goes by that we don't miss them. Holidays and birthdays are particularly unbearable. When we were putting our holiday decorations away that tragic year, I remember thinking I was putting Christmas away forever. In those first months, when I was consumed by unbearable pain, I would go outside to catch my breath and start humming whatever melody came to mind. One night when I couldn't sleep and was outside humming myself out of pain, I heard a soft crinkling sound. I turned on my porch light, and it was snowing. But it wasn't the usual snow—I have never seen snow like this. You could see every little snowflake and its design, shiny on one side and sparkling in the light like diamonds. That was the first time I felt a little peace; somehow I knew Nicholas was sending me a sign. When you get struck by a tragedy like the one that struck our family, you start paying attention to little things like you never had before. Once I saw a cloud in the sky that looked like a boy with open arms, as if he was trying to hug me. I was reminded of Ms. Gaynor's encouraging song and smiled as I thought, *so you're back from outer space*! Another time, during a huge storm, when there was nothing in the sky, a bright star appeared. At first I thought it was a helicopter, but it didn't move or make a sound; it just shone there for a few minutes and then disappeared into the storm.

Nicholas's final resting place is next to his grandfather's, and there is some comfort in knowing that they are together. A picture of Nicholas's soft and beautiful face is sketched on the gravestone, positioned to be visible even if you do not enter the cemetery grounds. I pass it almost daily.

On May 30, 2013, friends and family arrived at the cemetery to celebrate Nicholas's fifteenth birthday. We brought that many balloons with us to be released into the sky. As the balloons soared off in the distance, everyone noticed two balloons clinging together and straying to the left, while the others stayed their course. Was Nicholas telling us that he and Grandpa were on their own journey, making beautiful music in Heaven, and that they are always nearby, watching over all of us, even if we can't see them?

I could never express enough love and gratitude to all my friends for helping me survive, and, at times when I do listen to the radio, I find such powerful inspiration from "I Will Survive." Our friends picked us up when we crumbled, and they held us together with their love and support. My family and I would never have been able to make it through this awful, senseless tragedy without them, but now I can proudly say: "Oh, no, not I, I will survive!" I still hum, but the song has become a little happier!

OPENING THE DOOR

by Lynn Ruth Miller

It was my own personal horror story, and it happened in 1980.

I thought I was in paradise. I was living in a tiny house in Redwood City, California, with my three dogs. I could hardly believe how delightful my life had become. *This is what middle age should be,* I told myself. *I have finally found the road I need to follow.*

And then *it* happened.

It was ten o'clock, Saturday night, and I was hungry. I pulled out a turkey casserole from the refrigerator and put it in the oven. I plugged in the coffee grinder on the counter and spooned out some coffee beans. The tiny kitchen bubbled with the rich aroma of the casserole and the perking coffee.

And then I heard a man's footsteps outside.

I was furious. *Who does he think he is? Why does he have to cross my lawn to go next door? What's wrong with the street?*

I could hear the noise of his heels as he climbed over the fence, and I yanked the back door open. "You get out of there!"

He stood before me, a giant shadow in the doorway.

I froze.

I tried to push the door shut.

Too late.

He grabbed me by the collar and hit my face. My head snapped to one side, then the other. His features were stone.

"Why are you doing this?" I screamed.

My voice gurgled in my throat and my words died. I heard the thud of my body as it hit the floor, but I felt nothing.

I don't even know you. You are a horrible dream. Yes. That's it. Any minute I'll wake up and you'll be gone. You're that dill pickle I couldn't refuse. Do you understand? YOU ARE NOT REAL!

He struck me harder, again and again. I crashed into the Tiffany lamp. It clattered to the floor in a shower of broken blue glass. He used my shirt collar like a leash to lift me above the debris. His free hand smashed into my face again.

Once more I tried to scream, but my voice froze. My body was a bundle of white-hot pain. "Stop! *Stop!*"

The words rumbled like phlegm in my throat. My eyes filled with blood. It poured down my face and soaked my robe. I could taste it, acrid and bitter . . . awful.

Oh God, please make him quit. He's going to kill me.

He dragged me across the floor. My hips bounced against the hardwood boards. The jagged edges of the broken lightbulb ground into my legs. My slipper caught in the heat vent. I could feel my ankle twist as the shoe was wrenched from my foot.

My eyes refused to focus. The room whirled around me like a movie escaping from its reel. The dining-room table danced on marshmallow legs; the living-room couch squashed into a misshapen ball.

My robe twisted and my collar tightened around my throat. I gasped for air. My eyes bulged and my tongue filled my mouth like a saturated sponge. He pulled me into the bedroom. "No! *No!*"

At last my voice worked. It sounded like a warped record, a wild, banshee wail. I could hear it accelerate into knives of sound that sliced the blood-thickened air.

He stopped and threw my limp body against the wall. "Oh, the hell with it," he said.

I crumbled to the floor and skidded in a pool of blood.

He turned and wiped his hands on his pants. My blood spread across his black corduroy slacks. He tore open the bolted front door as if the locks were paper.

He disappeared.

I stumbled to the telephone. *Got to dial operator. Got to get help.*

I heard a cracked, frantic voice force itself out of my throat. "I've been attacked. Oh, help, someone. Help; 2925 Glendale. Hurry. Oh, please hurry."

Did that tinny sound come from *my* throat? Impossible. I dropped the receiver. I stared at red-streaked walls and carmine pools splattered across the floor. *Must clean it up . . . now.*

I staggered into the bathroom and wet a towel with cold water. My blood fell into the wet sink and spread like batik dye. I looked up into the mirror. Who was *that*?

A grotesque mask stared back at me. Its right eyebrow was pulled halfway to its hairline. Its nose was bent almost flat. Its mouth was frozen into a tight, pursed knot. Blood dripped down its lacerated chin.

That couldn't be me!

I got down on my knees and wiped up my footprints even as fresh blood fell to the floor. I held another rag to my face and washed the telephone. I soaked the stained towels in cold water. I rubbed them with soap that burned into the abrasions in my hands. I scrubbed until the stains had disappeared down the drain. I plugged the sink and soaked the towels again. Then I remembered dinner.

I forced myself to hurry into the kitchen. I turned off the oven.

Sirens.

"Thank God."

Through a veil of blood, I saw the two policemen enter. I staggered across the floor into their arms. I could smell the freshness of the outdoors on their rough wool coats.

"All right, lady," one officer said. "Try to calm down. Tell us exactly what happened. What did he look like? Have you ever seen him before?"

I shook my head. "He was dressed all in black like a silhouette and he smelled like . . ."

I frowned, puzzled. Then I nodded. "He smelled like jasmine, that's it . . . just like those bushes in Charlotte's front yard. He pushed his way through my back door and hit me."

I looked up at the men, and my eyes overflowed. I paused and swallowed. "Then he stopped."

"We're going to take you to the hospital. Someone needs to look at you."

I shook my head. "I want to go to bed. I'm so tired . . . *so* tired."

"Lady, your face won't wait. You might get some kind of infection. Where is your coat?"

Then the world went black. I returned home at four in the morning with stitches in my legs and forehead. I limped in pain. I leaned against the door and felt a hundred years old. The place was chaos. My heart walloped my ribs. I forced myself to concentrate on one action at a time. I moved slowly and methodically to set things right.

I propped a chair under the doorknobs of both doors and looked once more at the debris. I picked up my purse from the floor. I hung my coat in the closet. I scraped the dried blood from the carpet, the walls, and the telephone. I soaked more rags and rinsed out the ones I had used earlier. I looked at the door. It had scuff marks and streaks of dirt and blood. I sprayed it with Windex and it was clean. I tested the knob. The door was locked. I undressed and brushed my teeth.

I secured the chain lock.

I slept until Monday night. I felt swollen, as lumpy as a bag of potatoes. I went into the bathroom and looked in the mirror.

My eyes were swollen shut, my forehead bandaged, and my nose a crooked line. Black-and-blue smudges. Yellow, red, and purple marks, cuts, scabs. Pain. *Oh my Lord, how can one body ache this much?*

I turned away from the mirror and reached out to open the bathroom door. Suddenly the dogs burst into a cacophony of sound. They barked, yelped, and squealed. I took a deep breath. He was out there. He had come back to finish the job.

I felt myself shrink into a terrified knot and pulled away from the door. Then I stopped. I remembered my favorite song. It had come out two years before, and I used to hum it whenever I felt vanquished by an uncaring world. It was Gloria Gaynor's "I Will Survive." And that was when I knew what I had to do. I put my hand back on the doorknob. *That man has stolen forty-eight hours of my life from me,* I thought. *I am not giving him one minute more.*

And then I did the bravest act I have ever done before or since.

I opened the door and walked into the living room. Only the dogs were there.

"Come on, kids," I said to the dogs. "We're taking our walk."

The police asked me to file a report and I did, but I refused to allow myself to think that my attacker would reappear. The art of living is to cope with the unexpected. It is a waste of energy to live in fear that the unthinkable will happen. If I was to enjoy the rest of my life, I had to believe in my own powers of survival. I learned a huge lesson from that horrifying experience. I learned that I am strong enough to withstand the worst and rediscover the beauty that life offers.

I can survive. More than that, I can flourish.

ACKNOWLEDGMENTS

We would like to acknowledge and give thanks to the following individuals:

To my Lord and Savior, Christ Jesus, without whom no survival is possible.

To my mother, who taught me many lessons of survival that I only recently began to learn and appreciate.

To my manager, Stephanie Gold, whose consistent moral support, tireless scouting for resources, and dealing with every aspect of the book through its inception have been invaluable in bringing this project to fruition.

To my collaborator, Sue Carswell, reporter/researcher at *Vanity Fair*, whose personal dedication, expertise, insight, patience, and friendship, have been vital to this project.

To Colleen Sell, who launched us on our journey of finding contacts for stories and continuously supported and encouraged us through the process.

To Sue Carswell's agent, Claudia Cross, and a special thanks to *Vanity Fair* and especially the research department and its director, John Banta. Thanks also to Adam Nadler.

To my attorney, Gregory Cimino, who so skillfully guided us through the legal process.

To Nadine Brechner, who has been so very supportive with her contacts and resources.

To Gary M. Krebs, associate publisher and acquiring editor, Brilliance Publishing, who believed in the project and encouraged and supported us through it from its inception.

To the entire team at Brilliance Publishing and Amazon Publishing: Mark Pereira, managing director and publisher, Brilliance Publishing; Dan Byrne, managing editor; Tammy Faxel, business development; Kathlyn Schierbeek and her design team; Natalie Fedewa and Steve Woessner, sales; Brad Hill, producer; Grace Doyle, and Deborah Bass, publicity; Alicia Criner, marketing; Karen Upson, production; and Helen Cattaneo, author relations.

We would like to thank our publicists Meg McAllister, Heather Wagner-Reed, and Howie Simon.

To Robin Miles, my vocal coach, who was instrumental in preparing me for the narration of this book.

To Dino Fekaris and Freddie Perren, whose imagination and gifts as songwriters created the timeless song, "I Will Survive."

To Jenna Voorhees of Universal Music Licensing, who has stood by us and supported us through many projects, and had the insight and wisdom to know that "I Will Survive" would be the anthem for millions of people.

To all of the charitable organizations that believed in our mission and had the vision to know their impactful stories would go on to help so many.

To all of our contributors, who were brave and generous enough to share with us the private and intimate details of their stories and victories.

ABOUT THE AUTHORS

Grammy award-winning singer GLORIA GAYNOR took the music world by storm in the 1970s, striking platinum with her disco hit "I Will Survive." "I Will Survive" was the only song to earn a Grammy for Best Disco Recording and was one of only twenty-five songs inducted into the Grammy Hall of Fame in 2012. Gaynor has appeared on countless television and radio shows, received numerous national and international music and humanitarian awards, and continues to perform around the world for legions of fans. Her most requested song is, of course, "I Will Survive."

Coauthor SUE CARSWELL, author of *Faded Pictures from My Backyard* (Ballantine), is a reporter-researcher at *Vanity Fair* and has ghostwritten numerous books. She is a former executive and senior editor at Random House Inc. and Simon and Schuster, a former story producer for *Good Morning America*, and correspondent for *People* magazine.